THOMAS CAMPION AND THE ART OF ENGLISH POETRY

THOMAS CAMPION

AND THE ART OF ENGLISH POETRY

BY

THOMAS MacDONAGH, M.A. (1878 – 1916)
UNIVERSITY COLLEGE, DUBLIN

NEW YORK / RUSSELL & RUSSELL

FIRST PUBLISHED IN 1913 BY HODGES, FIGGIS & CO. LTD.
REISSUED, 1973, BY RUSSELL & RUSSELL
A DIVISION OF ATHENEUM PUBLISHERS, INC.
WITH THE PERMISSION OF HODGES, FIGGIS & CO. LTD., DUBLIN
L. C. CATALOG CARD NO: 72-84996
ISBN 0-8462-1685-X
PRINTED IN THE UNITED STATES OF AMERICA

TO
ROBERT DONOVAN
PROFESSOR OF ENGLISH LITERATURE, UNIVERSITY COLLEGE,
DUBLIN

THIS BOOK IS DUTIFULLY INSCRIBED

PREFACE

THIS book was written and presented by me in 1911 as a thesis for the degree of Master of Arts at University College, Dublin. It is printed now without change. Planned as a dissertation on Thomas Campion's *Observations in the Art of English Poesie*, it developed from Chapter V on into something like a complete treatise on English Metrics and Rime, deriving from Campion's work, and following my division of English verse into the two species of Song-verse and Speech-verse. In addition to the ordinary subjects of works on English metres, my survey, in this portion of the book, has included the relations of music and metre, of quantitative verse and accentual verse, of song, speech and chant, the function of pause in a *staccato* language like English, the differences between quantity and accent in English and in the Classics, the origin of rime, its function and its use.

The present work deals only with Song-verse. I hope to publish in the course of the next year or two an analysis of the other species.

To Mr. T. S. Omond, author of three important works on English metrics and English metrists, to

Thomas Campion and the Art of English Poetry

Messrs. A. H. Bullen and S. Percival Vivian, editors of Campion's works, and to Mr. R. W. Chapman, Secretary of the Clarendon Press, Oxford, I owe my thanks for permission to quote from necessary authorities. The text of the poems in Chapter IV is that of Mr. Bullen's *editio princeps*. Several of the facts of Campion's life, recorded by me in Appendix A, have been discovered by Mr. Vivian, and published in his complete Clarendon Press edition of my poet's works.

To Mr. Vivian I owe, in another sense, one word more. Replying to a letter of mine about his denial of Campion's Irish origin, he writes: "I think you will have difficulty in tracing Campion's origin to Ireland. I spent much time in following up that clue, but without a particle of success; and all the parish registers and other evidence which I adduce, prove that the family was well rooted in Hertfordshire at an early date." I give him his voice here, as his letter arrived too late for me to add this as a note to Chapter II.

To Professor Robert Donovan and to the Reverend Professor George O'Neill I tender my thanks for advice, encouragement and approval.

UNIVERSITY COLLEGE, DUBLIN,
December 1912.

CONTENTS

CHAP.		PAGE
I.	INTRODUCTORY	1
II.	CAMPION'S LIFE AND WORKS	7
III.	THE BEGINNINGS OF ENGLISH PROSODY: CAMPION'S "OBSERVATIONS"	17
IV.	A SELECTION FROM THE ENGLISH POEMS OF THOMAS CAMPION	23
V.	ENGLISH NUMBERS	41
VI.	SONG, SPEECH AND CHANT	50
	RÉSUMÉ OF CHAPTERS V AND VI	59
VII.	MUSIC AND METRE—QUANTITATIVE VERSE AND ACCENTUAL VERSE	60
VIII.	ACCENT, QUANTITY, PAUSE, EQUIVALENCE	75
IX.	RIME	92
APPENDIX A.	SUMMARY OF KNOWN FACTS RELATING TO THOMAS CAMPION	115
APPENDIX B.	THE BEGINNINGS OF ENGLISH PROSODY	118
APPENDIX C.	SYNOPSIS OF "OBSERVATIONS"	119
APPENDIX D.	SAMUEL DANIEL AND HIS "DEFENCE OF RYME"	122
LISTS OF AUTHORITIES		127

Thomas Campion and the Art of English Poetry

CHAPTER I

INTRODUCTORY

A man of faire parts and good reputation.
SAMUEL DANIEL.

"THE great period of English poetry," says Arthur Symons, "begins half-way through the sixteenth century, and lasts half-way into the seventeenth. In the poetry strictly of the sixteenth century, before the drama had absorbed poetry into the substance of its many energies, verse is used as speech, and becomes song by way of speech. Music had come from Italy, and had found for once a home in England. It was an age of music. Music, singing, and dancing made then, and then only, the 'Merry England' of the phrase. And the words, growing out of the same soil as the tunes, took equal root. Campion sums up for us a whole period, a perfect craftsman in the two arts."

Thomas Campion was a contemporary of William Shakespeare, and his equal in age from birth to death—

Thomas Campion and the Art of English Poetry

Shakespeare, 1564–1616; Campion, 1567–1620. Others of his equals, in this sense, were his opponents in the metrical controversy, Samuel Daniel (1562–1619); Joshua Sylvester (1563–1618), to whom one of his most beautiful songs was for long attributed; Michael Drayton, born in 1563; Christopher Marlowe, born in 1564; and Thomas Nashe (1567–1601), his friend and admirer, honoured by him in his Latin verses. Ben Jonson and John Donne, great poets, the powerful influences of the next generation, were six years younger than Campion. This matter of dates may at first sight seem to count for little, but, to draw a comparison from the main part of this dissertation, the unit, the essential, is the period; the poet articulates the period. This was a period of music and power, and each good poet of it was the higher and stronger for the height and strength of his contemporaries. The phenomenon occurred again in England at the beginning of the nineteenth century, and then the wave came double-crested—Wordsworth (b. 1770), Scott (b. 1771), Coleridge (b. 1772), Byron (1788–1824), Shelley (1792–1822), Keats (1795–1821).

Two or three other such lists include all but a few of the great writers of the English language. There are some that are heard like a single word in the night, but in general the history of literature is like a line of verse, "a succession of sounds and silences," each sound syllabled, vowelled.

Introductory

Campion was, then, a close contemporary of Shakespeare; yet in only one contemporary record that we know of are the two poets mentioned together. In no record of their time can they have been mentioned with greater honour, "laudati a laudato viro." Camden, in his *Remaines of a Greater Worke concerning Britaine*, published in 1605, passes from "some Poeticall descriptions of our aunchient Poets" to his contemporaries: "If I would come to our time, what a world could I present to you out of Sir Philipp Sidney, Ed. Spencer, Samuel Daniel, Hugh Holland, Ben. Jonson, Th. Campion, Mich. Drayton, George Chapman, John Marston, William Shakespeare, and other most pregnant witts of these our times, whom succeeding ages may justly admire." With the exception of Hugh Holland, who reminds one of the Hugh O'Lara of Lady Gregory's *Image*, one succeeding age or another has admired them indeed. With that one exception, Thomas Campion is last to receive his meed. From 1619 to 1814 there is a blank in his bibliography. The first edition of Palgrave's *Golden Treasury* knew him not. Later editions have wronged him by the inclusion of some of his inferior work and by the exclusion of some of his most lovely songs.

In 1814 he had appeared in Sir Egerton Brydges' *Excerpta Tudoriana*. The following year saw the first modern reprint of his *Observations in the Art* of *English Poesie*, in Hazlewood's *Ancient Critical Essays*. Then again a long blank till 1887, which gave us *Lyrics from the Song Books*. The year 1889 brought the *editio princeps* of his collected works, edited by Mr. A. H. Bullen. Campion had then been dead two hundred and sixty-nine years. There are at present two important editions of his works—Mr. Bullen's and Mr. Percival Vivian's—and three or four minor cheap editions. Now that after such long waiting he has won the admiration of a succeeding age, his fame is certain to stand, poised delicately on slight, graceful, strong foundations of beauty. We recognise in Campion a true poet, as truly a poet for his age as was his contemporary Shakespeare for all time. He is a poet of the Elizabethan song-books. His highest praise is that he is the best poet of the song-books.

For students of the art of English poesy his work has a further rare interest and value. He was a metrist in theory and practice. Here again, in theory, he was of his age; in practice he was a precursor. He was a scholar in an age of much wrong-headed learning. He was a sweet singer in an age of song. He wrote more poems in Latin than in English. He wrote of English verse as if it were imitation Latin verse. He tried to train himself to a foreign mode of poetic speech. He strove to write by rule and not by ear. He " whose commendable rimes had given

Introductory

to the world the best notice of his worth,"[1] was at much pains to show that the natural graces of English verse were vain and unworthy. He became, as Daniel laments, "an enemy of rime." He railed against "shifting rime, that easy flatterer," against "the fatness of rime"—he, whose rimes and cadences, composed both before and after his railing, are unsurpassed in English song. But his ear triumphed. He followed his rule only a little way. Soon again he "tuned his music to the heart." He was too true a lyric poet to tune it to the false tones of the erring schoolmen.

And even in his railing and in his error his acute perception gives him glimpses of truth. His *Observations* is by far the ablest of the Elizabethan treatises on quantitative verse.[2] If the Elizabethan age was the greatest in matter of poetic achievement, it was so because it was free from self-consciousness. Campion, thinking much more highly of his English sapphics and of his Latin epigrams, referred to his lovely "Airs" as "after the fashion of the time, ear-pleasing rimes without art." Shakespeare's notes were to the greatest poet of the next age "native wood-notes wild," ear-pleasing, without art. But Campion and Milton sang native wood-notes too, in spite of what they thought to be their knowledge of

[1] Samuel Daniel, *A Defence of Ryme*, 1603.
[2] T. S. Omond, *English Metrists*.

higher things, in spite of the Renaissance and its sequel. Shakespeare the dramatist spoke through his masks the nervous, eager, living language of his tongue. Shakespeare unlocked his heart—or did not [1]—with the sonnet key which he found to his hand, imported and adapted by his immediate predecessors. Shakespeare, the lover of music, " warbled his native wood-notes wild," careless, most probably ignorant, of quantity, and stress, and " isochronous periods," and all the rules of English metrics—of all but what makes the best knowledge and creates ear-pleasing rimes without art, concealing art.

Campion, like Milton, was a musician. It would be interesting to trace the effect of Milton's musical knowledge on his verse, not merely on his verse of organ voice, but on the lyric measures of *Arcades* and *Comus* and *Samson Agonistes*. In Campion the effect is obvious and evident. His verse suggests music. All his lyrics are " airs," songs set to music, published with their tunes. Always in his verse he " chiefly aimed," as he says, " to couple words and music lovingly together." He is essentially a craftsman of the two arts.

[1] Wordsworth: " . . . With this key Shakespeare unlocked his heart." Browning: "Did Shakespeare? If so, the less Shakespeare he!"

CHAPTER II

CAMPION'S LIFE AND WORKS

Sweet Master Campion.
Marginal in a copy of William Covell's *Polimanteia* (1595).

We ought to maintain as well in notes as in action a manly carriage.
CAMPION.

I HAVE relegated to an appendix my detailed account of the life of Thomas Campion. Here, before proceeding to treat of the poet's works, I deal in passing with two points which do not fit into a chronological enumeration of the facts of his life. Very little is known with certainty of the grandson of John Campion of Dublin. I hope that further investigations will throw some new light on his ancestry. Mr. Percival Vivian, his most recent and most thorough biographer, brushes aside the Irish connection of his family, and fixes John Campion the elder as a Hertfordshire man, who "may have visited Ireland on some venture, commercial or otherwise, or held a paltry office there." The minutes of the Parliament held in the Middle Temple in 1565 do not give colour to this surmise. Therein the poet's father, John Campion, is described as "son and heir of John Campion of Dublin, Ireland, deceased." There were Campions in Ireland at the time. The name, which appears to have been formerly pronounced Champion in Ireland and England, was one of the English forms of the Irish name O'Crowley, in Gaelic O Cruaidhlaoich, the descendant of the Hard Warrior, or Champion. It is quite common to the present day in Kilkenny and Queen's County. This, however, is not the place to go into the question of the poet's pedigree or to examine in detail Mr. Vivian's conclusions and inferences concerning his family. In the appendix I have given in chronological order the accepted facts.

The poet was born on Ash Wednesday, 12th February, 1567, and christened the following day at St. Andrew's Church, Holborn, of which parish his father was assistant or vestryman. Dr. Jessop in *The Dictionary of National Biography*, Mr. A. H. Bullen in his editions of Campion, and Mr. Vivian in his small " Muses' Library " edition, have been at some pains to prove the poet a Catholic. They have drawn inferences from the religion of his most intimate friends, the Mychelburnes, Sir Thomas Monson, and others; from the possibility of relationship between him and Edmund Campion, the Jesuit martyr, " the Pope's Champion "; from the fact that he did not proceed to a degree in Cambridge, though he was known to have been of the university;[1] and from his attacks on the

[1] "It was quite usual at this period for Englishmen who had conscientious objections to the religious tests enforced at both universities to abstain from matriculating or taking a degree."— PERCIVAL VIVIAN *in " Muses' Library " Edition.*

Campion's Life and Works

Puritans. Researches made by Mr. Vivian or at his instance have now made it known that he belonged to Peterhouse, Cambridge; his not taking a degree argues nothing as to his faith. It is certain that his family adhered to the religion by law established. While satirising the Puritans—in itself no proof at the time of Catholicism—he hailed Elizabeth as "Faith's pure shield, the Christian Diana," and in his Latin poem "Ad Thamesin (de Hyspanorum fuga)" wrote :

> "Nec Romana feret purgatis Orgia fanis
> Reffluere, aut vetitas fieri libamen ad aras.
> O pietas odiosa deo, sclerataque sacra,
> Quae magis inficiunt (damnosa piacula) sontes."

Mr. Vivian in his complete edition of Campion recants his former pleading, and writes the poet down a moderate Anglican.

In the very first poem that we know for certain to be his, Campion is already "a curious metrist," in the phrase of W. E. Henley. This poem, Canto Primo of *Poems and Sonets of Sundry Other Noblemen and Gentlemen*, printed with a surreptitious edition of Sidney's *Astrophel and Stella* in 1591, and reprinted in *A Book of Airs*, 1601, is indeed amongst the best examples in English of the beauty of hovering or wavering rhythms. Canto Secundo of the same set is an experiment in classical rhythms :

"Whát faíre / pómpe haue I spíde / óf glitteríng / Ladíes,"

an accentual imitation of the Latin Asclepiad Minor.

Of these I shall treat in the body of this dissertation. Here they are worth noting as indicating already the double bent of the poet—to classical theorising and imitation on the one hand, and on the other to freedom of lyric singing, won from practice of music and the lute.

Campion was twenty-four when these first-fruits of his genius appeared. It is probable that other poems of his were well known in the literary circles of London, for in 1593, eight years before the publication of *A Book of Airs*, George Peele had already addressed him as :

> "Thou
> That richly cloth'st conceite with well made words,
> Campion."

In 1595 was published his first acknowledged work, *Thomæ Campiani Poemata*, Latin poems which established him, in the opinion of his contemporaries, as one of the greatest " Englishmen being Latine poets."

In 1601 came *A Booke of Ayres, set foorth to be song to the Lute, Orpherian, and Base Violl, by Philip Rosseter, Lutenist*. The book is dedicated by Rosseter, on the authority of Master Campion, to Sir Thomas Monson ; and in the dedicatory epistle half the airs are spoken of as of Campion's " own composition, made at his vacant houres, and privately emparted to his friends, whereby they grew both publicke, and (as coine crackt

Campion's Life and Works

in exchange) corrupted." The words of all the songs are Campion's, and by these alone he takes rank as the first poet of the Elizabethan song-books. The singing quality of most of these songs, the grave, solemn music and earnest poetry of some, the metrical originality, the lovely grace and variety of the rime, mark their author as the friend and master of this kind of poetry.

And yet his next work showed him an enemy of rime. In 1602 he published his *Observations in the Art of English Poesie*, dedicated, strangely enough, to the famous author of the Induction to the *Mirrour for Magistrates*, one of the finest masters of English rimed verse.[1]

In 1607 appeared Campion's *Masque in Honour of Lord Hayes and his Bride*. This is followed by a comparatively long silence, broken only by an occasional complimentary reference to the "rare Doctor." The silence ends in 1613, his *annus mirabilis*. The *Masque for Lord Knowles*, the *Lords' Masque*, *Songs of Mourning*, *Two Books of Airs*, and the *Masque for the Marriage of the Earl of Somerset*, are the harvest of that year. The masques are full of good things, always

[1] Thomas Sackville, Lord Buckhurst and Earl of Dorset (1536–1608), part author of the first English tragedy, *Gorboduc* or *Ferrex and Porrex*. The "Induction" is a stately poem, a solemn monotone pealing in a sombre hall. "It forms," says Hallam, "a link which unites the school of Chaucer and Lydgate with *The Faery Queen*. Mr. Saintsbury styles Sackville the "author of some of the finest rime-royal in the language."

of songs that take one with lovely first lines. Few
poets have excelled Campion in winning openings of
song. "Advance your choral motions now," in the
Lords' Masque, sings itself; other measures dance
themselves, heel and toe :

> " Come ashore, come, merry mates,
> With your nimble heels and pates." [1]

The first of the *Two Books of Airs* contains " Divine
and Moral Songs." " His devotional poetry," says
Mr. Bullen, "impresses the reader by its sincerity.
To fine religious exaltation Campion joined the true
lyric faculty, and such a union is one of the rarest of
literary phenomena. In richness of imagination the
man who wrote When thou must home to shades of
underground' and 'Hark, all you ladies that do
sleep' was the equal of Crashawe ; but he never failed
to exhibit in his sacred poetry that sobriety of judg-
ment in which Crashawe was sometimes painfully
deficient." [2] And in this poetry of his again is the
sound of the harp with the words ; and, like David's
harp in Bacon's fine phrase, it has " as many hearse-
like airs as carols." The poem " Where are all thy
beauties now, all hearts enchaining ? " with its solemn
three-lined stanzas and double rimes, has something

[1] *Masque for Marriage of Earl of Somerset.*

[2] I give this as I find it. "Sobriety" generally produces dulness,
but "sobriety" is not really a quality of Campion's poetry.

Campion's Life and Works

of the fall of the " Dies Iræ," and the great, earnest music of doom.

> " Thy rich state of twisted gold to bays is turnéd !
> Cold, as thou art, are thy loves, that so much burnéd !
> Who die in flatterers' arms are seldom mournéd."

Of even a higher mood are " Never weather-beaten sail " and " Come, cheerful day, part of my life to me," while " To music bent is my retiréd mind " and " Tune thy music to thy heart " have the grace of simple singing rhythm that gave to the lyrics of that age a great part of their ineffable charm.

The second of the two books, the *Light Conceits of Lovers,* has some things for which Campion thought it right in the dedication to apologise, but enough of unsullied song to outshine all the rest. " What harvest half so sweet is," " The peaceful western wind," " There is none, O none but you," are masterpieces of melody.

In 1614 Campion published the *Masque for the Marriage of the Earl of Somerset,* composed and produced in the previous year. During the two following years he was in trouble, implicated in the plot for the murder of Sir Thomas Overbury, though quite innocent of guilt. In 1617, the *Third and Fourth Books of Airs.* In these again is an ever new variety of rhythm and rime and colour, if we may call it so. It is impossible ever to speak of the " subject " of a poem of Campion's ; it is never with him a matter of theme and treatment, as modern reviewers would have it. His gift was song—" to sing and not to say," as Swinburne claimed of Collins—and his achievement, " full-throated ease." Mr. Bullen has drawn attention to the extraordinary and ever-recurring " difference " of Campion. On opposite pages of his *Third Book of Airs* are " Now winter nights enlarge " and " Awake, thou spring of speaking grace ! mute rest becomes not thee ! " and again, " Shall I come, sweet love, to thee ? " and " Thrice toss these oaken ashes in the air."

The finest songs of these two books are also the most interesting metrically.[1] And yet, when one has said so, the thought of some others, simple and uncarved, gives one pause.[2]

Here may be mentioned poems which are with good reason attributed to him, and some occasional verses. The most interesting of the latter is the hymn to Neptune—" Of Neptune's empire let us sing "—with its one strange sliding line in each verse. Of the former class, and almost certainly his, is an exquisite poem published by Richard Alison in his *Hour's Recreation in Music* (1606), " What if a day, or a month, or a year ? " For the rest, complimentary verses, dedicatory verses, verses prefixed to the works

[1] " Kind are her answers," " Break now my heart and die," " Fire, fire," " Every dame affects good fame," " To his sweet lute," " Love me or not."

[2] " Sleep, angry beauty," " Never love unless you can," " Turn all thy thoughts to eyes."

of the poet's friends, and the like, though always graceful and occasionally distinguished, are to us less interesting than one little poem attributed to Campion by Mr. Bullen on grounds of style alone—a poem which brings for the first time into English verse a cadence which in our age, joined to an artifice of rime not unknown to Campion,[1] has won, or largely helped to win, for one poem a place in a most select class, beside Gray's *Elegy* and Coleridge's *Ancient Mariner*.[2] One hears the music of Fitzgerald's *Rubaiyat* in these lines:

> " The rarer pleasure is, it is more sweet,
> And friends are kindest when they seldom meet.
> Who would not hear the nightingale still sing,
> Or who grew ever weary of the spring ? "

In 1618 was published *The Airs that were sung and played at Brougham Castle in the King's Entertainment*, almost certainly written by Campion, though composed by others. The song for a dance, " Robin is a lovely lad," has all his quaintness and musical dexterity. It was probably in the same year that he issued *A New Way for making Four Parts in Counterpoint*, a very technical treatise, long a standard book,

---

[1] The inclusion of an unrimed line in a rimed stanza.

[2] It is difficult to find a definition to cover the *Elegy*, the *Ancient Mariner*, and the *Rubaiyat;* yet for other reasons than comparative similarity of length they must occupy a place together in English poetry.

and frequently reprinted. It afforded a rule of thumb for the harmonisation of tunes with simple concords.

In 1619 Campion published a splendid volume of Latin verse, containing four hundred and fifty-three epigrams, thirteen elegies, and one long poem. Judging from his prefaces, Campion considered these Latin poems his great work. To us their interest lies in their introducing us to the poet's literary circle. He addresses epigrams to William Camden, Charles Fitzgeoffrey, the three Mychelburnes, William Percy, Thomas Nashe, John Dowland, Edmund Spenser, Sir John Davies, and others.

In the second book of the *Epigrams*, No. 23, we get a description of the poet himself—a lean man, envious of the fat :

> " Crassis invideo tenuis nimis ipse, videtur
> Satque mihi felix qui sat obesus erit . . ."

On one day, March 1st, 1620, Campion made his will, died, and was buried. His sole legatee was his lifelong friend, Philip Rosseter ; his place of burial, St. Dunstan's in the West, Fleet Street.

CHAPTER III

THE BEGINNINGS OF ENGLISH PROSODY :
CAMPION'S " OBSERVATIONS "

How now Doctor Champion, musicks and poesies stout Champion,
Will you nere leave prating ?
　　　　　　From MS. commonplace book of a Cambridge
　　　　　　　　　student (*circa* 1611).

Is this faire excusing ?　O, no, all is abusing.
　　　　　　　　　　　　　　　CAMPION.

CAMPION'S *Observations in the Art of English Poesie,* which appeared in the year 1602, is the third in order of time among the metrical treatises of importance published in English. It is, in the opinion of that most competent judge, Mr. T. S. Omond, by far the ablest of the Elizabethan treatises on quantitative verse. In 1575 had appeared George Gascoigne's *Certayne Notes of Instruction in English Verse*, and in 1589 George (or Richard) Puttenham's (or another's) *The Art of English Poesie*. Other works,[1] half a dozen or so, had looked in at the door of prosody, but only these two had entered and stayed. Even they scarcely affect Campion's work and the matter in hand ; they affect it, indeed, rather less than some

[1] See Appendix B for list of works.

Thomas Campion and the Art of English Poetry

of the minor works, such as William Webbe's *Discourse of English Poetrie*, from which he takes points, or the famous correspondence between Gabriel Harvey and Edmund Spenser about English accent and quantity. Nearly all the writers of the age who interested themselves in the grammar of the craft were infected with a passion for the " reform " of English verse, to remake it nearer to the heart's desire of classical schoolmen. And as the schoolmen in both France and England, ignorant of scientific philology, blundered at almost every step in their spelling reforms, so these prosodists, ignorant of the true nature of quantity and accent, blundered. The reformation failed because poets sing by ear and not by rule. The language was true to itself in its poetry. It is a joy to find Campion's worthy antagonist, the poet Samuel Daniel, proclaiming in his *Defence of Ryme* the duty of a literature to the genius of its language.[1] Yet Campion himself is a greater joy. He writes, now shrewdly, incisively, suggestively, of English verse, now all wrongly, led astray by his reverence for accent and his love of quantity, as he understood it. Always he writes with energy and earnestness, always with the zeal and ardour of a poet with music in him. The voice that breaks into those exquisite lyric openings of song after song in

[1] I have made a special appendix (Appendix D) for Daniel and his *Defence*. He was not only " a good poet in his day," but a splendid master of prose. I give some excerpts from his book.

Campion's "Observations"

his *Book of Airs* is the same voice that presses so eloquently another business in the *Observations*—in the prose arguments of his treatise. For what are these "versings" of his, quoted as examples (or, indeed, as I suspect, the first springs of the whole train)—what are they to his rimed songs:

"There is none, O, none but you,"

or:

"Awake, thou spring of speaking grace!"—

How can one choose among them?

I can well believe that Campion, in his youth certainly just the poet to be quickly responsive to all the influences of his age, wrote some at least of the unrimed poems printed by him in his *Observations*, before he thought of setting up as a prosodist. It must always be a strong temptation to poets of metrical originality to show their contemporaries that their innovations are not due to ignorance of the conventional ways of verse, and are not arbitrary irregularities. This is not to say that such innovations and such metrical irregularity are conscious, studied, arranged beforehand. One cannot repeat often enough the truth that the true poet sings by ear and not by rule, his ear no doubt formed by the music of the verse of his language, but his own, hearing that music in his own way, directing his tongue to utter his music in his own way. Afterwards, the rule. The good conventional critics of all the ages have reproved poets who made new music, have declared it no music. It must always be a strong temptation to the poets of the new melody to reply, to explain, to lay down rules of justification. If they do so, they probably will leave unsaid more than they say; they will easily give wrong explanations. If he is to make a new music, the poet in a man must be far in advance of the grammarian. In some men the poet and the grammarian have little to do with each other. Such a man was Edgar Allan Poe;[1] such a man was Wordsworth;[2] such a man was Campion. In him the poet had much to do with Master Campion, who "in his vacant hours" composed music, who "neglected these light fruits as superfluous blossoms of his deeper studies."[3] He "chiefly aimed," as he said, "to couple words and notes lovingly together." He never published a lyric without its musical setting. In him the grammarian, the author of the *Observations*, had to do with "sweet Master Campion" of Cambridge,

---

[1] See Poe's *Rationale of Verse* and some of his essays and "marginalia." He resembles Campion not a little, in his incisiveness when right, and in his ingenuity when wrong.

[2] See the famous preface to the *Lyrical Ballads*. "Most of our attempted explanations of artistic merit (which contains elements non-moral and non-intellectual) are incomplete and misleading. Among such explanations must be ranked Wordsworth's essays. It would not be safe for any man to believe that he had produced true poetry because he had fulfilled Wordsworth's conditions."—F. W. H. MYERS.

[3] Rosseter's dedication to *A Book of Airs*.

Campion's "Observations"

the "scholarly learned," the "gentlemanlike qualified,"[1] with Thomas Campianus who had "attained renown and place among Englishmen, being Latine poets."[2] Thomas Campion, student of Gray's Inn, was one or the other at different times. Thomas Campion, doctor in physic, scarcely intruded into either personality.

In Appendix C I give a full synopsis of the *Observations*. Here I serry the points which to a modern metrist are most interesting and suggestive. They fall under twelve headings :

1. The inter-relation of accent and quantity in English, always confused by Campion (Chapter I *et passim*). Quantitative poetry in English. Rules of quantity in Latin and English (Chapter X).

2. Music and metre (Chapter VII *et passim*).

3. Rime. Its "inaptness." Origin. Rime in Latin (Chapter II).

4. Alliteration—barely glanced at (Chapter II).

5. " English numbers " in general (Chapter III).

6. English and Latin verse compared (Chapter IV).

7. " Sliding " of verse (Chapters III and IV).

8. Pause—Campion's " rests " or " natural breathing-places" (Chapter IV).

9. Normal line-period measurable (Chapters IV and X).

[1] William Covell's *Polimanteia*.   [2] Meres' *Palladis Thamia*.

10. Metrical equivalence (Chapter IV *et passim*).

11. Long-lined and short-lined English verse. The hexameter in English (Chapters III, V, *et passim*).

12. Iambic and trochaic verse, anapæstic and dactylic, " rising and falling accents "—Campion's term (Chapter IV *et seq.*).

In following chapters I deal with these points, but not, of course, in the order given here.

CHAPTER IV

A SELECTION FROM THE ENGLISH POEMS OF THOMAS CAMPION

From "A Book of Airs"

The cypress curtain of the night is spread,
And over all a silent dew is cast.
The weaker cares, by sleep are conquered :
But I alone, with hideous grief aghast,
In spite of Morpheus' charms, a watch do keep
Over mine eyes, to banish careless sleep.

Yet oft my trembling eyes through faintness close,
And then the Map of Hell before me stands ;
Which ghosts do see, and I am one of those
Ordain'd to pine in sorrow's endless bands,
Since from my wretched soul all hopes are reft
And now no cause of life to me is left.

Grief, seize my soul ! for that will still endure
When my craz'd body is consum'd and gone ;
Bear it to thy black den ! there keep it sure
Where thou ten thousand souls dost tire upon !
Yet all do not afford such food to thee
As this poor one, the worser part of me.

FOLLOW your saint, follow with accents sweet!
Haste you, sad notes, fall at her flying feet!
There, wrapp'd in cloud of sorrow, pity move,
And tell the ravisher of my soul I perish for her love:
But if she scorns my never-ceasing pain,
Then burst with sighing in her sight and ne'er return again!

All that I sung still to her praise did tend;
Still she was first; still she my songs did end:
Yet she my love and music both doth fly,
The music that her Echo is and beauty's sympathy.
Then let my notes pursue her scornful flight!
It shall suffice that they were breath'd and died for her delight.

BLAME not my cheeks, though pale with love they be;
The kindly heat unto my heart is flown,
To cherish it that is dismay'd by thee,
Who art so cruel and unsteadfast grown:
For Nature, call'd for by distressed hearts,
Neglects and quite forsakes the outward parts.

But they whose cheeks with careless blood are stain'd,
Nurse not one spark of love within their hearts;
And, when they woo, they speak with passion feign'd,
For their fat love lies in their outward parts:
But in their breasts, where love his court should hold,
Poor Cupid sits and blows his nails for cold.

A Selection from the English Poems

> WHEN the god of merry love
> As yet in his cradle lay,
> Thus his wither'd nurse did say:
> " Thou a wanton boy wilt prove
> To deceive the powers above;
> For by thy continual smiling
> I see thy power of beguiling."
>
> Therewith she the babe did kiss;
> When a sudden fire outcame
> From those burning lips of his,
> That did her with love inflame.
> But none would regard the same:
> So that, to her day of dying,
> The old wretch liv'd ever crying.

WHEN thou must home to shades of underground,
And there arriv'd, a new admired guest,
The beauteous spirits do engirt thee round,
White Iope, blithe Helen, and the rest,
To hear the stories of thy finish'd love
From that smooth tongue whose music hell can move;

Then wilt thou speak of banqueting delights,
Of masques and revels which sweet youth did make,
Of tourneys and great challenges of knights,
And all those triumphs for thy beauty's sake:
When thou hast told these honours done to thee,
Then tell, O tell, how thou didst murder me.

Thomas Campion and the Art of English Poetry

THOUGH far from joy, my sorrows are as far,
And I both between;
Not too low, nor yet too high
Above my reach, would I be seen.
Happy is he that so is placed,
Not to be envi'd nor to be disdain'd or disgraced.

The higher trees, the more storms they endure;
Shrubs be trodden down:
But the Mean, the Golden Mean,
Doth only all our fortunes crown:
Like to a stream that sweetly slideth
Through the flow'ry banks, and still in the midst his
    course guideth.

SHALL I come, if I swim? wide are the waves, you
    see:
Shall I come, if I fly, my dear Love, to thee?
Streams Venus will appease; Cupid gives me wings;
All the powers assist my desire
Save you alone, that set my woful heart on fire!

You are fair, so was Hero that in Sestos dwelt;
She a priest, yet the heat of love truly felt.
A greater stream than this, did her love divide;
But she was his guide with a light:
So through the streams Leander did enjoy her sight.

A Selection from the English Poems

WHETHER men do laugh or weep,
Whether they do wake or sleep,
Whether they die young or old,
Whether they feel heat or cold ;
There is, underneath the sun,
Nothing in true earnest done.

All our pride is but a jest ;
None are worst, and none are best ;
Grief and joy, and hope and fear,
Play their pageants everywhere :
Vain opinion all doth sway,
And the world is but a play.

Powers above in clouds do sit,
Mocking our poor apish wit ;
That so lamely, with such state,
Their high glory imitate :
No ill can be felt but pain,
And that happy men disdain.

FROM "TWO BOOKS OF AIRS"

THE man of life upright,
  Whose cheerful mind is free
From weight of impious deeds
  And yoke of vanity ;

The man whose silent days
   In harmless joys are spent,
Whom hopes cannot delude
   Nor sorrows discontent;

That man needs neither tow'rs,
   Nor armour for defence,
Nor vaults his guilt to shroud
   From thunder's violence;

He only can behold
   With unaffrighted eyes
The horrors of the deep
   And terrors of the skies;

Thus, scorning all the cares
   That fate or fortune brings,
His book the heav'ns he makes,
   His wisdom heav'nly things;

Good thoughts his surest friends,
   His wealth a well-spent age,
The earth his sober inn
   And quiet pilgrimage.

A Selection from the English Poems

NEVER weather-beaten sail more willing bent to shore,
Never tired pilgrim's limbs affected slumber more,
Than my wearied sprite now longs to fly out of my troubled breast.
O come quickly, sweetest Lord, and take my soul to rest!

Ever blooming are the joys of heav'n's high Paradise,
Cold age deafs not there our ears nor vapour dims our eyes:
Glory there the sun outshines; whose beams the blessed only see.
O come quickly, glorious Lord, and raise my sprite to Thee!

COME, cheerful day, part of my life to me:
    For while thou view'st me with thy fading light,
Part of my life doth still depart with thee,
    And I still onward haste to my last night.
Time's fatal wings do ever forward fly:
So every day we live a day we die.

But, O ye nights, ordain'd for barren rest,
    How are my days depriv'd of life in you,
When heavy sleep my soul hath dispossest,
    By feigned death life sweetly to renew!
Part of my life in that, you life deny:
So every day we live a day we die.

JACK and Joan they think no ill,
But loving live, and merry still;
Do their week-days' work, and pray
Devoutly on the holy day:
Skip and trip it on the green,
And help to choose the Summer Queen;
Lash out, at a country feast,
Their silver penny with the best.

Well can they judge of nappy ale,
And tell at large a winter tale;
Climb up to the apple loft,
And turn the crabs till they be soft.
Tib is all the father's joy,
And little Tom the mother's boy.
All their pleasure is Content;
And care, to pay their yearly rent.

Joan can call by name her cows,
And deck her windows with green boughs;
She can wreaths and tuttyes make,
And trim with plums a bridal cake.
Jack knows what brings gain or loss;
And his long flail can stoutly toss:
Makes the hedge, which others break;
And ever thinks what he doth speak.

Now, you courtly dames and knights,
That study only strange delights;

A Selection from the English Poems

Though you scorn the homespun gray,
And revel in your rich array :
Though your tongues dissemble deep,
And can your heads from danger keep ;
Yet, for all your pomp and train,
Securer lives the silly swain.

WHAT harvest half so sweet is
As still to reap the kisses
   Grown ripe in sowing ?
And straight to be receiver
Of that which thou art giver,
   Rich in bestowing ?
Kiss then, my Harvest Queen,
   Full garners heaping !
Kisses, ripest when th' are green,
   Want only reaping.

The dove alone expresses
Her fervency in kisses,
   Of all most loving :
A creature as offenceless
As those things that are senseless
   And void of moving.
Let us so love and kiss,
   Though all envy us :
That which kind, and harmless is,
   None can deny us.

Where shall I refuge seek, if thou refuse me?
In you my hope, in you my fortune lies,
In you my life! though you unjust accuse me,
My service scorn, and merit underprize:
  O bitter grief! that exile is become
  Reward for faith, and pity deaf and dumb!

Why should my firmness find a seat so wav'ring?
My simple vows, my love you entertain'd;
Without desert the same again disfav'ring;
Yet I my word and passion hold unstain'd.
  O wretched me! that my chief joy should breed
  My only grief and kindness pity need!

FROM "THE THIRD BOOK OF AIRS"

Kind are her answers,
But her performance keeps no day;
Breaks time, as dancers
From their own music when they stray.
All her free favours
And smooth words wing my hopes in vain.
O did ever voice so sweet but only feign?
Can true love yield such delay,
Converting joy to pain?

Lost is our freedom,
When we submit to women so:
Why do we need them
When, in their best they work our woe?

A Selection from the English Poems

There is no wisdom
Can alter ends, by Fate prefixt.
O why is the good of man with evil mixt ?
Never were days yet call'd two,
But one night went betwixt.

Now winter nights enlarge
The number of their hours ;
And clouds their storms discharge
Upon the airy tow'rs.
Let now the chimneys blaze
And cups o'erflow with wine,
Let well-tun'd words amaze
With harmony divine !
Now yellow waxen lights
Shall wait on honey love
While youthful revels, masques, and Courtly
    sights,
Sleep's leaden spells remove.

This time doth well dispense
With lovers' long discourse ;
Much speech hath some defence,
Though beauty no remorse.
All do not all things well ;
Some measures comely tread,
Some knotted riddles tell,
Some poems smoothly read.

The summer hath his joys,
And winter his delights;
Though love and all his pleasures are but toys,
They shorten tedious nights.

THRICE toss these oaken ashes in the air,
Thrice sit thou mute in this enchanted chair;
And thrice three times, tie up this true love's knot!
And murmur soft, "She will, or she will not."

Go burn these pois'nous weeds in yon blue fire,
These screech-owl's feathers and this prickling briar;
This cypress gathered at a dead man's grave;
That all thy fears and cares an end may have.

Then come, you Fairies, dance with me a round!
Melt her hard heart with your melodious sound!
In vain are all the charms I can devise:
She hath an art to break them with her eyes.

    FIRE, fire, fire, fire!
Lo here I burn in such desire
That all the tears that I can strain
Out of mine idle empty brain
Cannot allay my scorching pain.
Come Trent, and Humber, and fair Thames!
Dread Ocean, haste with all thy streams!
    And if you cannot quench my fire,
    O drown both me and my desire!

A Selection from the English Poems

    Fire, fire, fire, fire!
There is no hell to my desire.
See, all the rivers backward fly!
And th' Ocean doth his waves deny,
For fear my heat should drink them dry!
Come, heav'nly show'rs, then, pouring down!
Come you, that once the world did drown!
    Some then you spar'd, but now save all,
    That else must burn, and with me fall!

COME, O come, my life's delight,
    Let me not in languor pine!
Love loves no delay; thy sight,
    The more enjoyed, the more divine:
O come, and take from me
The pain of being depriv'd of thee!

Thou all sweetness dost enclose,
    Like a little world of bliss.
Beauty guards thy looks: the rose
    In them pure and eternal is.
Come, then, and make thy flight
As swift to me, as heav'nly light.

NEVER love unless you can
Bear with all the faults of man:
Men sometimes will jealous be,
Though but little cause they see;

And hang the head, as discontent,
And speak what straight they will repent.

Men that but one saint adore,
Make a show of love to more :
Beauty must be scorn'd in none,
Though but truly serv'd in one :
For what is courtship but disguise ?
True hearts may have dissembling eyes.

Men when their affairs require,
Must a while themselves retire :
Sometimes hunt, and sometimes hawk,
And not ever sit and talk.
If these and such like you can bear,
Then like, and love, and never fear !

FROM "THE FOURTH BOOK OF AIRS."

Ev'ry dame affects good fame, whate'er her doings be,
But true praise is Virtue's bays which none may wear but she.
Borrow'd guise fits not the wise, a simple look is best ;
Native grace becomes a face, though ne'er so rudely drest.
Now such new found toys are sold, these women to disguise,
That before the year grows old the newest fashion dies.

A Selection from the English Poems

Dames of yore contended more in goodness to exceed
Than in pride to be envi'd, for that which least they
    need.
Little lawn then serv'd the Pawn, if Pawn at all
    there were ;
Homespun thread, and household bread, then held out
    all the year.
But th' attires of women now wear out both house
    and land ;
That the wives in silks may flow, at ebb the good
    men stand.

Once again, Astrea, then, from heav'n to earth descend,
And vouchsafe in their behalf these errors to amend !
Aid from heav'n must make all ev'n, things are so
    out of frame ;
For let man strive all he can, he needs must please
    his dame.
Happy man, content that gives and what he gives,
    enjoys !
Happy dame, content that lives and breaks no sleep
    for toys !

    THERE is a garden in her face,
    Where roses and white lilies grow ;
    A heav'nly paradise is that place,
    Wherein all pleasant fruits do flow.
    There cherries grow, which none may buy
    Till " Cherry ripe " themselves do cry.

> Those cherries fairly do enclose
> Of orient pearl a double row;
> Which when her lovely laughter shows,
> They look like rosebuds fill'd with snow.
> Yet them nor peer nor prince can buy
> Till "Cherry ripe" themselves do cry.
>
> Her eyes like angels watch them still;
> Her brows like bended bows do stand,
> Threatening with piercing frowns to kill
> All that attempt, with eye or hand,
> Those sacred cherries to come nigh
> Till "Cherry ripe" themselves do cry.

To his sweet lute Apollo sung the motions of the spheres;
The wondrous order of the stars, whose course divides the years;
    And all the mysteries above:
    But none of this could Midas move,
  Which purchas'd him his ass's ears.

Then Pan with his rude pipe began the country wealth t' advance,
To boast of cattle, flocks of sheep, and goats on hills that dance;
    With much more of this churlish kind,
    That quite transported Midas' mind,
  And held him rapt as in a trance.

This wrong the God of Music scorn'd from such a sottish judge,
And bent his angry bow at Pan, which made the piper trudge :
    Then Midas' head he so did trim
    That every age yet talks of him
    And Phœbus' right-revenged grudge.

    TURN all thy thoughts to eyes,
    Turn all thy hairs to ears,
    Change all thy friends to spies,
    And all thy joys to fears :
        True love will yet be free,
        In spite of jealousy.

    Turn darkness into day,
    Conjectures into truth,
    Believe what th' envious say,
    Let age interpret youth :
        True love will yet be free,
        In spite of jealousy.

    Wrest every word and look,
    Rack every hidden thought,
    Or fish with golden hook ;
    True love cannot be caught.
        For that will still be free,
        In spite of jealousy !

FROM "DAVISON'S POETICAL RHAPSODY."

Of Neptune's empire let us sing,
At whose command the waves obey:
To whom the rivers tribute pay,
Down the high mountains sliding:
To whom the scaly nation yields
Homage for the crystal fields
    Wherein they dwell:
And every sea-god pays a gem
Yearly out of his wat'ry cell
To deck great Neptune's diadem.

The Tritons dancing in a ring
Before his palace gates do make
The water with their echoes quake,
Like the great thunder sounding:
The sea-nymphs chant their accents shrill,
And the sirens, taught to kill
    With their sweet voice,
Make ev'ry echoing rock reply
Unto their gentle murmuring noise
The praise of Neptune's empery.

Note.—I have omitted from this selection some good poems quoted by me in subsequent chapters.

CHAPTER V

ENGLISH NUMBERS

Poesy in all kind of speaking is the chief beginner and maintainer of eloquence, not only helping the ear with the acquaintance of sweet numbers, but also raising the mind to a more high and lofty conceit.

CAMPION.

TOWARDS the end of his latest book, *English Metrists in the Eighteenth and Nineteenth Centuries* (1907), the ablest of English metrists, Mr. T. S. Omond, regrets that he and his fellow-workers have as yet failed to establish a system of English prosody good for all verse. At the same time he announces his confidence that an authoritative and accepted synthesis will come, and that it will be not more but less complex than the known systems. This is, in the first place, a proclamation of proud humility, worthy of Samuel Daniel himself.[1] Mr. Omond, who has much reason to be "in love with his own mystery," with his originality, with his scientific exactness, with his care in analysis and inquiry, is not so far in love with them as almost any disciple of his would be on his behalf. And it is so easy for a discoverer to believe that he has reached his India or his Ultima Thule. For the

[1] *Cf.* passage quoted in Appendix D.

rest, Mr. Omond's sentence is at once a promise and a challenge to younger metrists. And there is still more of challenge in his concluding paragraph : " We may reasonably look with expectation to what the next few years will bring. If the whole truth has not yet been reached, it is now recognised as attainable." If I think that I have discovered a truth hitherto at least unnoticed or unproclaimed, I claim it with proper diffidence. It is in itself, as it seems to me, so obvious a thing that I did not regard it as a discovery till I found that there is no mention of it in the many metrical treatises which I have studied.[1] I do not know if it may prove a key to the whole truth, but I am confident that it will serve as a sure key to open at least the outer casket.

Words may be uttered in three distinct ways by the human voice. They may be spoken, or sung, or chanted. They are generally either spoken or sung, the chant being a mode of utterance lying somewhere between the two extreme modes—nearer, I think, to song than to speech.

Music is always definitely rhythmic, with stress recurrent at regular intervals.[2]

[1] The German metrist, Saran, distinguishes two species of English verse, "alternating" and other. His method of division, however, differs from mine, and has not the same foundation of music and speech.

[2] Mr. Carl Hardbeck of Belfast has shown in a lecture that in certain Irish tunes, set to Irish words, the music goes out of its way, as it were, to follow the varying expression of the words, which

English Numbers

Prose speech has its own rhythm, but it is not the rhythm of music.

Prose, then, is uttered by the speaking voice, not by the singing voice. It may be said that prose can be sung. The sentence which forms my last paragraph can certainly be sung to a tune, but in that case song changes it into verse.

> " Prose speech has its own rhythm,
> But it is not the rhythm of music."

This will happen almost always in a passage of prose. One sentence will have such a rhythm as to be capable without change of being read as verse. But the rhythm is not repeated in the next sentence. Herein—in the fact that sentence after sentence changes rhythm—lies the essential difference of prose from verse. In verse there is a recurrence ; in prose there is no recurrence. In music there cannot be a tune without recurrence ; therefore prose, as prose, cannot be sung to a tune. Prose, then, is in general spoken. Prose may be chanted without having violence done to its rhythm or sense. Obviously verse also may be chanted.

As there is recurrence in music and in verse, it

in an Irish song are all important. The tunes played by him in the regular way without the words were inferior in beauty to the tunes sung wandering with the wavering words of the poems. But, of course, this proves nothing against the rhythmic regularity of airs. I shall have to refer to this matter again in connection with the poetry of Mr. Yeats and others.

would seem at first that all verse can be set to a tune without violence or "wrenching." This does not prove to be the case. Milton's *Paradise Lost*, for instance, could not be so set.

> "Of man's first disobedience and the fruit
> Of that forbidden tree, whose mortal taste
> Brought death into the world and all our woe . . ."

This does not go to a tune, line by line; nor does it run in lines of regular rhythmic recurrence. Nowhere in Milton's poem will be found a set of lines that run long enough on the same stress construction to make an air. Let us take now some lines of ten syllables from a different kind of poem, one of Sir William Davenant's:

> "The merchant bows unto the seaman's star,
> The ploughman from the sun his season takes;
> But still the lover wonders what they are
> Who look for day before his mistress wakes."

Here the rhythm is the rhythm of an air of music. The difference between these lines and Milton's is not merely the difference of rime. These lines are lyric in the strict sense; Milton's are quite another thing. Milton's lines lose by being set to music, even to a recitative. The words get their due and varying value in being rightly read. Nothing of that kind, at least, is lost to Davenant's lines in being sung; other things are gained, and the music gains by the words. In Milton's line—

> "Brōught death into the world and āll our wōe"

English Numbers

there are three long-vowel syllables and two natural pauses. The long syllables do not of necessity occur regularly, in the even places or the like. The " weight and due proportion," to use one of Campion's terms, are at least better brought out in reading than in singing. And the great point is that this weight and due proportion constitute the essential metrical quality of the line, that it differs from a lyric line in being governed by these.

My thesis is that there are two main kinds of verse in English, song-verse and speech-verse.

Song-verse has its origin in music.
An air of music may be sung on one syllable, thus :

> " la la la la—la la la la
> la la la—la la—la la la
> la la la la la—la la la
> la la la la la—la la la."

or it may be sung on words (a combination of vowels and consonants) and pauses :

> " Come live with me and be my love,
> And we will all the pleasures prove
> That hills and valleys, dales and fields,
> Or woods or steepy mountain yields."

Song-verse may be spoken or chanted, but it still suggests an air. And this is one of the most striking qualities of Campion's songs, that they not only suggest the tune, but at times even the instrument to which the poet sang, the throbbing of the lute, and at times an undertone as of other strings in concord. Song-verse of what may be called the primary order, made to the lyre, calls for its air. Miss Janet Dodge, in her note on Campion's music prefixed to Mr. Bullen's reprint of his *editio princeps*, speaks of the melody of one of his songs, " Awake, thou spring of speaking grace," as springing to meet the idea. The idea had called for it. How the old airs of Shakespeare's songs —of " It was a lover and his lass," of " O mistress mine "—carol the words ! And what a different and finer thing is that song of Marlowe's, which I have quoted, when sung to its air ! One thinks of how Izaak Walton heard it two hundred and eighty years ago : " It was a handsome milkmaid, that had not attained so much age as to load her mind with any fears of many things that will never be, as too many men often do ; but she cast away all care, and sung like a nightingale : her voice was good, and the ditty fitted for it ; it was that smooth song which was made by Kit Marlow, now at least fifty years ago."

Speech-verse has its origin in human speech as distinguished from song. It is a development of speech through oratory and the like, not from or through vocal music.

This distinction between two kinds of verse was probably recognised in the classic languages. The

English Numbers

sermo pedestris or *Musa pedestris* of Horace was speech-verse, the *carmen* song-verse. He speaks of both kinds as *poemata*.[1] " Prose rhythm," says a writer in the *Encyclopædia Britannica*, " imitates the measured movement of the body in stately speech. Renan thought the ancient *poetry* of the Hebrews founded on this."

English song-verse is rhythmical—that is, it consists of equal units, uniform in duration.[2] Prose has its rhythm, but the units are not uniform. In song-verse there is a regular recurrence of the units. This does not necessarily mean a recurrence of similar words, or of syllables similar in accent or quantity, though that is common. The foot is not the unit. Of what, then, does the unit consist ? Not exactly of words or syllables, for these vary, but of something fixed in which syllables may be " embedded." The units are time-spaces, isochronous periods.

Song-verse is made up of a succession of such units or periods, syllabled and silent.

Syllables make up words. Words have accent. Words have quantity.

Lines and sentences are combinations of words, generally with some pauses between. " A verse is a series of sounds and silences." [3]

Song-verse, then, is made up of rhythmic lines con-

[1] *Cf.* Horace: *Ars Poetica*, 91–99 ; *Sermonum Lib.* ii. 6.

[2] In this paragraph I follow closely Mr. Omond's statement at the beginning of his *Study of Metre.* I limit it, however, to song-verse.

[3] J. M. Robertson, M.P., in the *English Review*, June 1911.

taining a number of units, the units being isochronous periods. The recurrence of these periods or time-spaces is marked by word-accent. Pause, Campion's "rests," and quantity are other components. In all: (1) rhythm, (2) time-space units, (3) accent, (4) quantity, (5) pause. The unit, when filled, syllabled and stressed, or silent, may for convenience be called a foot, the foot being equivalent to the bar in music, to which song-verse closely corresponds.

To this kind of verse, besides the poems usually called lyric, belong in general short-lined poems, or poems in long lines which can be divided into short lines. For instance, Campion's poem—

"Never weather-beaten sail / more willing bent to shore,"

might be printed in four-feet and three-feet lines. The example of a long-lined lyric which springs to the mind is the famous Elizabethan song, "Since first I saw your face." On looking it up now in Chappell's *Old English Popular Music*, I find it printed in short lines:

"If I admire or praise you too much
That fault you may forgive me."

(The old air of this, by the way, is "coupled lovingly" with the words. All the syllables of "praise you too much" are duly honoured.)

Song-verse is not only of simple but of complex harmonies, so is not limited to short poems in a single rhythm.

English Numbers

The components of speech-verse at first sight would seem to be the same as those of song-verse, but on examination one finds that the lines are not made up of isochronous periods. Rhythm, accent, quantity and pause, stand. A new component—weight, to give it Campion's name—is of all importance. There is, of course, a time norm. The lines are equal in time, but vary internally, ebbing and flowing according to the pressure of weight, in a way unknown in song-verse. In this dissertation I deal only with the latter, meaning to make a detailed analysis of speech-verse on another occasion. Under the heading of speech-verse fall blank verse, the heroic couplet, and in general all verse of length in time corresponding to lyric lines of five units or more. I use the term "length in time" to avoid ambiguity. Some verse of double rising or falling measure, like "The Assyrian came down like a wolf on the fold," with four units, has twelve syllables to the line, two more than the five-foot decasyllabic line, yet the latter is longer in time.

This division of English verse into two species is not arbitrary, or founded merely on foot-rule measure, short and long. The same natural law of rhythm which has established the English pentameter, and refused similarly to establish verse of seven or of nine stresses, is responsible.

CHAPTER VI

SONG, SPEECH AND CHANT

The Apothecaries have Books of Gold, whose leaves, being opened, are so light as that they are subject to be shaken with the least breath; yet rightly handled, they serve both for ornament and use. CAMPION.

Men of moment, rationals and irrationals.

CAMPION.

I HAVE spoken of song-verse and speech-verse as the two extreme modes. Now, to satisfy all objections to dogmatism, comes, up the middle way, the mode exceptional, mixed verse, in which the speech element and the song element combine.

This is akin to chant. It owes its origin either to chanting to the harp or lyre, or to the invention of tone-deaf poets and of poets who, though high-musical, compose their verse through chanting rather than through song. In dealing with questions of this kind it is in general improper to examine together things unlike, more improper still to measure with an ell such altitudes as the ecstasy and gravity of poetic utterance. Yet, for fear of misunderstanding, it may be well here to institute a brief comparison between song- and speech-verse.

Song, Speech and Chant

Lyric poetry, the sheer clear lyric singing of ecstasy, may reach a height and intensity ineffable.

The poetry of speech-verse at its greatest, in some passages of Shakespeare, of Milton, of Keats, of Wordsworth, in English, has a loftiness and power, a depth and a height, that make it seem and be the noblest expression of human thought.

Lucretius in his speech-verse, grave, passionate, towering, sublime; Catullus in his lyric, with his " clear and terrible simplicity," lucid, intense, rapturous, " burning upward to his point of bliss," or else bitter, poignant, in agony, or else impersonal, objective, exquisite, quaint, dainty, singing; Wordsworth at his highest all that Lucretius is, Shelley all that Catullus is—these are set on different, equal pinnacles, apart.

And not less lofty is the peak to which are lifted other poets whose poems show the evolution of a third species of verse. Their Parnassus rises between the other two.

A person with a musical ear cannot chant a poem set to a tune, while that tune is being played on an instrument. I have lately tested this. I have used a lyre in preference to a piano in going through old English and Elizabethan airs for the purposes of this dissertation. I have found it pleasant and strange and new to sing to the simple instrument, in immediate

Thomas Campion and the Art of English Poetry

contact with the strings, the old songs, "Sumer is icumen in," Campion's "What if a day or a month and a year," Shakespeare's "O mistress mine" and "It was a lover and his lass," and other old songs mentioned previously. I have then, while playing the tune, tried to chant, as I understand chanting and as I usually chant verse. I have found that my voice always broke into the melody. Mr. W. B. Yeats, being quite tone-deaf—or perhaps, I should say, tune-deaf—though of fine ear for all sound values other than pitch, could, I am sure, continue his chanting, not only undisturbed, but probably aided by the rhythm of the tune on the lyre. It is this chanting quality in his verse and in the verse of some others, joined to a wandering rhythm caught from Irish traditional music, that has informed a new species of verse. It is chant-verse, overflowing both song-verse and speech-verse. For not only does something of the word reverence of chanted speech unstress the lyric beat of this poetry, but something of the musical quality of chant lightens and changes the weight of its speech-verse.

Mr. Omond is puzzled quite by Mr. Yeats' speech-verse—

"The mountain of the gods, the unappeasable gods "—

and asks: "Are such lines metrical?" Mr. Omond's theories do not cover speech-verse. If he had taken this line for a lyric line, he would have found little

Song, Speech and Chant

difficulty with it. It really is speech-verse, coloured by a strong tint of lyric through chant.

I do not think of speech-verse as mere speech, necessarily unmusical in any sense of the word. It is verse because it is something else than ordinary speech, as song-verse is verse because it is something else than pure music. The speech quality in speech-verse lies in the weight and procession of the words. Milton's and all good speech-verse is built up in sentences, not in lines or in fractions of lines. The metrical unit is the line—that is, the lines are equally long in time. This makes and requires a larger scope and management than song-verse, in which the units are the periods in the line.

Song-verse and speech-verse meet in chant, but they meet from opposite directions.

The tone-deaf poet is not necessarily inferior to the musician as poet. Indeed, except in comparison with some musical poets of extraordinary metrical ability, who know "a music that transcends tune," the tone-deaf poet rather gains than loses by his not recognising airs. It is thought that blindness may make the sense of hearing more acute in an individual. The tone-deaf poet is able to chant his verse as I can well believe that Homer chanted his, in the days before our modern music evolved, changing a tone up or a tone down with the emotion of the words, not making a tune and not keeping on a monotone like a musician when chanting.[1] Coventry Patmore in his *Essay on Metrical Law* remarked that the tattoo of a knuckle upon the table will lose most, if not all, of its rhythm if transferred to a bell. "The drum," he says, "gives rhythm, but the clear note of the triangle is nothing without another instrument, because it does not admit of an imagined variation."

On the other hand, of course, poets with musical ear are not incapable of attaining the same metrical music as tune-deaf poets. The poet with ear only for obvious effects and for obvious rhythms will be so, whether he be tune-deaf or not. A poet like Campion is not so. His very musical power led him beyond the obvious, and made him the "curious metrist," the first initiator of delicate wandering speech effects in song-verse, which are now found in a new manifestation, as it were, in the poets to whom I have referred.

I have just now, since writing the above, had an opportunity of testing in a rare way some of my theories. Mr. George W. Russell ("Æ") visited me, and at my request recited in his way some poems—Shelley's "Hymn of Pan," W. B. Yeats' "O colleens, kneeling at your altar rails long hence," and passages

[1] A writer in the *Quarterly Review* (July 1911) holds that the musical element in verse (or poetry, as he has it) absorbs the whole attention of a mind peculiarly sensitive to effects of sound. He instances Tennyson as a poet of exquisite ear for verse music while tune-deaf.

Song, Speech and Chant

from Milton, Keats (*Hyperion*), Walt Whitman, Swinburne, and others, together with the sixteenth century poem (or imitation sixteenth century), " As ye came from the Holy Land of Walsinghame," and some pieces of his own.

He recited these from memory, untroubled by printed text, and in all of them he gave to each word and to each line its due value and verse music. Mr. Russell is tone-deaf. He chants verse on a few notes, rising and falling with the emotion. Mr. James Stephens, who came in also, and I, both of musical ear, found that when we did not merely *say* verse, we chanted it on a monotone, or, if we chanted otherwise, the changes that we made seemed to be directed by musical ideas or memories.

Mr. Russell suffers in no way, and, I think, rather gains, in his chanting of verse by his deafness to tune. The same is true, as I have already said, of Mr. Yeats, who some time ago read for me in a chanting voice some of Coventry Patmore's poems from *The Unknown Eros*. These two poets, Æ and W. B. Yeats, with a few others, have in their lyric verse a quality of chanted speech rather than of barred music. Mr. Yeats in his speech-verse has a quality of lyric chant.

Besides the species of verse in which song and speech qualities combine and meet in chant, the song-tone colouring the speech and the speech-tone colouring the song, there is a chant species of song-verse with no proper speech element. This is probably older than song-verse pure and simple, and goes back to the time when poets chanted long narrative poems to the harp. It is certain that the Greek bards did not merely *say* or recite epic poems. It is certain that Irish bards did not. The very thought that they sang thousands of lines to anything like a tune repeated over and over, is intolerable. The troubadour was a poet-musician, who composed airs to his songs, properly so called; but the *popular* epic poems of North and South France are known to have been chanted. The *artistic* epic, or personal narrative poem, when it came, was recited—a thing worth noticing. And it is of interest, too, to notice that the artistic epic runs in couplets, while the popular epic is in strophes or tirades.

To this chant-verse in English belong ballad metre and the four-stress measure used by narrative poets from Chaucer to Coleridge and Scott, and from Scott to the present day. Chant-verse of this kind may be said to have lost position as a separate genus; it is now merged in the other two—metrically in song-verse, and, as to manner of delivery, in speech. Still it sounds on truly, and, to the harps of bards who know its measure, distinctively. To suit unaccompanied delivery of it there has grown up, in Ireland at least, a kind of narrative folk-music, song not chant,

Song, Speech and Chant

consisting of short airs in one part. When I was a child I knew an old woman who sang many ballads and stories in verse. She had only three or four tunes, and exceedingly monotonous tunes they were, and very much alike. They went with the ballad metre of her stories, four-stress lines and three-stress lines alternately—very " licentiate " lines, Campion would have called them, for they varied in number of syllables, in accentuation, in all but the regularity of stress. I used to shudder with delight when she came to a line in which she had to fit in half a dozen syllables to one stress—not that I thought of them then as syllables or stresses, or rightly understood what was the charm. One of these songs was a version of the Scotch ballad " Edward " (" Why does your brand sae drap wi' blude, Edward, Edward ? ") ; but I have now forgotten the words of this and the others, and all but snatches of the airs. They early gave me an idea that there is a definite species of narrative music, as distinguished from song music ; I think it a development of chant songwards.

This latter kind of chant then goes with song-verse metrically, having the same components, so that its existence does not interfere with my division of English verse into two main species.

Campion has set to music some speech-verse poems, and, being Campion, has done it with wonderful grace.

Thomas Campion and the Art of English Poetry

Miss Dodge, who has written of his music, is haunted by the melody of "Thrice toss these oaken ashes in the air," the words of which were originally written as a sonnet. Even more memorable as poetry is No. **xx.** of *A Book of Airs*:

> " When thou must home to shades of underground,
> And there arrived, a new admiréd guest,
> The beauteous spirits do engirt thee round,
> White Iope, blithe Helen, and the rest. . . . ."

How different in species this is from the poem before it, " Hark, all you ladies " ! How much finer chanted than sung—chanted as speech-verse, tolling out its rich contrasted rimes and ordered vowels, unchanged by scaling notes !

Résumé of Chapters V and VI

Two species of English verse: song-verse and speech-verse.

Song-verse built up of words in lines. The units, isochronous periods, in which syllables are "embedded." The time of the periods marked by word-stress.

Components: rhythm of time-space periods, stress, quantity, pause.

Rime may be added as an ornament, and is generally found in English song-verse.

Speech-verse built up of words in sentences, written in isochronous lines, governed by "weight."

Components: line-rhythm, stress, quantity, pause.

Rime may be added as an ornament, and may be used, as in song-verse, for binding and contrasting.

Between song-verse and speech-verse, and across the two, is chant-verse, not in itself metrically a separate species.

CHAPTER VII

MUSIC AND METRE—QUANTITATIVE VERSE AND ACCENTUAL VERSE

If Music and sweet Poetry agree,
As they must needs, the sister and the brother . . .
RICHARD BARNFIELD.

But above all the accent of our words is diligently to be observed, for chiefly by the accent the true value of syllables is to be measured.
CAMPION.

IN all the arts it is of essential importance to observe and to preserve due respect of the medium. Painting that tries to produce statuesque effects, to imitate sculpture on canvas, sculpture that tries to produce pictorial effects, music that tries to produce speech effects, verse that tries to produce the effects of pure sound, may all of them attain a certain effectiveness, but they are all something out of joint. Each art has its due medium, either colour, or form in marble or bronze, or pure sound, or expressive language. The writer who said of Shelley that his proper medium was not speech but music was wrong ; but still he showed that he recognised the difference of medium. Shelley expressed or interpreted in words an ecstasy

Music and Metre

of intuition intangible to most others. He used the language of vision and intuition to give to kindred intelligences images of his concepts. Language is in general a symbolic code for the transmission of the conceptions of the senses, a code of words which are the names of things or which express the relations of these things to one another. Music is a code of a different kind. Music also may express our ideas of things seen and heard—may make us hear the waves upon the shore, or see trees torn by the tempest. But this is by the way, and is included in a wider scope. Music in general expresses things which cannot be expressed in any of the other codes. Language expresses things which cannot be expressed in music. Language which borders on the music of pure sound, as it is claimed that Shelley's language does, expresses things akin to music concepts, but still in the province of language. And the difference between the two mediums is distinct. In both there is sound, in both rhythm. In music sound goes up and down an extended scale, and it is pure sound. Words are spoken on a few notes, and syllables are not pure sound. In music there is a great freedom of equivalence : a semibreve, not to go further up, may be replaced by two minims, or by four crotchets or eight quavers, and so on to semi-demi-semiquavers ; or by combinations of these. And these have, so to speak, vertical scope of pitch as well as horizontal scope of quantity. On the other hand, in quantitative verse a long syllable may be replaced by two shorts; in accentual verse a foot may be of three syllables or of two, or at times of one; a rising stress may be substituted for a falling stress—and there equivalence ends. Finally, the words in verse are chosen primarily not for their musical effect, but for their meaning.

A single note of music conveys nothing. A single word has still its sense. A short passage of music can convey little or nothing, whereas a few words may express something of great import. Campion, Shakespeare, Coleridge, Beddoes, Shelley used musical effects in verse to express more than mere words would have conveyed. The French symbolists have aimed at inventing a new music-language code. To do so thoroughly it would have been necessary to invent vocables that are not already occupied by meanings. It is possible to construct verse of known words full of such wonderful music as would of itself arouse emotions that the sense of the words would not arouse; but it is next to impossible for one who knows the language in which such verse is written not to follow the meaning of the words, or, if the words are void of meaning, not to be perplexed or alienated by its absence. With one who does not know the language, or who is not sufficiently familiar with it to follow it when spoken, the case is different. I have read for a friend of mine a poem of Maeterlinck's in French,

Music and Metre

and have found that it aroused in him the emotion of mysterious loss suggested also by the sense. When I translated the poem into English, the glamour was gone. Tolstoi, in *What is Art?* bitterly attacks such a use of language; but whereas on the one hand some of the symbolistic poets go to the extreme of nonsense in their compositions, Tolstoi surely goes to the extreme of too common a common sense in his condemnation of them.

In both music and verse there are sound and rhythm. In music there is a wide scope of pure sound. In verse there is, by comparison, a narrow scope. But then verse has all the sound-varieties of vowels and consonants and their combinations. And, in addition, verse uses the medium of expressive language. The qualities of this medium, technically speaking, are the subject of my analysis.

The master errors of the Elizabethan " versers " were the confusion between quantity and accent in general, and the confusion between the quantity of Latin words and of English words. Campion and the others who tried to introduce into English what they thought to be classical measures, took it for granted that things true, as they understood them, of Latin were true universally. This misunderstanding marred all their reasoning.

In the first place, Latin rules of quantity by position cannot be applied to English. In Latin some vowels

Thomas Campion and the Art of English Poetry

are long, and are long always. Some vowels are short; but if they are followed by two or more consonants (I state the rule generally), they find themselves in a long syllable. I do not consider it correct to say, as is always said, that the *vowel* is lengthened by position. A syllable consisting of a vowel sound with two consonant sounds or a double consonant sound is long. In Latin, as in modern Italian, the two " c's " and the two " l's " of *bacca* and *villa* were pronounced: the spelling was orthography. English spelling can be no guide to quantity. If any rule of the Latin kind were to be formulated, it would probably be the direct opposite of the Latin rule: it might be laid down that a double consonant shortens the preceding vowel, and that a vowel followed by another vowel is generally long, not short as in Latin. It would be useless to go into the matter further—to show the wrongness of Campion's quantities in his final chapter, "gŏīng," "pīttĭe," and the rest. The wrong track is wrong from the first step.

In the second place, a long syllable in English or in Latin (supposing word-stress in Latin) may not be the stressed syllable. The first line of Virgil's *Æneid* occurs to all writers on prosody as an obvious example:

" Ármă vǐrūmquĕ cănō Trójaē quī prímŭs ăb ōrīs."

If word-stress occurred at all in this line, it fell on the first syllables of the dissyllabic words, and the first

Music and Metre

syllables of " virum " and " cano " are short. Other syllables in that case are long and unstressed. Most readers of English would read this Latin line as if it were *accented* thus :

" Árma virúmque canó Trojǽ qui prímus ab óris,"

stressing the first syllables of the feet. And indeed it is very difficult for one accustomed only to accentual languages to read it aright with speech intonation. It is hard to win the voice from its accentual habit of hammering the stressed syllable. The late Mr. W. J. Stone denies that stress lengthens a syllable, and thinks that its function is rather to preserve it from conversational shortening. He goes even further, and says that it preserves it from lengthening. Mr. Stone is generally sound, but has generally been misunderstood. I hesitate in disagreeing from him, yet I do feel that to my ear, and in my reading of accentual verse, stress certainly has a real lengthening effect. At all events, English speakers have at all times confused the long syllable with the stressed syllable, and read that Latin line wrongly. If the line be chanted on a monotone in marked time, the quantity will be observed. In that case the word-stress will be lost. That both were observed by Romans is regarded as certain by almost all the writers whose works I have consulted on the matter, Mr. Stone among them.[1] I

[1] The great Cambridge scholar Munro and Dr. Blass are powerful exceptions, and have held, I believe, the true lamps to our feet.

do not believe it. How they could have observed pitch and accent superadded to quantity I cannot imagine. The primary difficulty for us is that in English we use accent to mark rhythm, leaving to quantity what Mr. Omond calls an ancillary function, whereas the Romans used quantity to mark the rhythm, and indicated the pitch of the syllables by the rise and fall of the voice. That they did so mark the pitch is known from the fact that in the earliest codex of Virgil's works, a manuscript of the fourth century, in the Laurentian Library at Florence, are neumes [1] as guides to the reader or reciter.

Mr. Stone in his pamphlet [2] quotes a correct Virgilian hexameter written by James Spedding:

" Sweetlў cŏmēth slūmbēr clōsīng thĕ o'erwēārĭĕd ēyelīd,"

and shows that if a couple of changes are made, thus:

" Sweetlў fạlleth slūmbēr clōsīng thĕ wēārĭĕd ēyelīd,"

there are two shocking false quantities.

Mr. Stone defines the difference between ancient and modern metres: "In the one the verse scans by quantity alone, the accent being used only as an ornament, to avoid monotony. In the other the functions are exactly reversed, the accent deciding

[1] "Neumes" (*neuma*, Greek for a nod or sign, not *pneuma*, a breathing), derived from the Greek accents, used to represent the degrees of the scale, unsystematised till the eleventh century. \, grave, indicated fall, /, rise, ~ indicated fall on one syllable.

[2] The title is *Classical Metres in English*.

Music and Metre

scansion, the quantity giving variety. The final result on the ear I believe to be very much the same, but whereas we tend (theoretically) to accent exclusively and are only unconsciously affected by quantity, with the ancients the position was reversed." I do not understand what he means by saying that the final result on the ear is the same. It will be seen that he omits all mention of classical pitch; and later in his essay he is at much pains to disprove a statement by Dr. Blass (in his *Pronunciation of Ancient Greek*) that in Greek accent consisted of word-pitch, not voice-stress. Previously, as I have already said, he had stated that accent in English does not lengthen the syllable at all. Yet when one reads his model quantitative line, one either makes certain syllables, like the " ing " of " closing," noticeably long, in order that the verse may run like a classical hexameter and not with the snap of final unaccented syllables in English, or one reads it :

" Swéetly cómeth slúmber, clósing the‾o'erwéariëd éyelid,"

unconscious indeed of the quantity.[1] Quantity has a place and use in English, but not this use.

On the whole it may be said that classical comparisons are of little avail, and have been of much hindrance in English prosody. Campion and most of his contemporaries were convinced that all dignity

[1] To him the "ing" followed by "th" made a long syllable.

and right rule derived from the ancients. Yet, strange to say, where the saying of an ancient would have led them right, they refuse to follow. In the first chapter of his *Observations* Campion shows that Terence "confounded music and poetry together." This did not lead him to the right conclusion, that with the ancients musical rhythm was the same as verse rhythm, as was certainly true of Greek.[1] His own knowledge that length of notes does not govern musical rhythm, would then have taught him that there was an essential difference somewhere. He thought that modern verse should conform to the rules of classic verse, as he took it for granted that ancient music and modern were the same. As almost all other writers on music and metre have fallen into this error, it may be well to enter here more than a summary contradiction of it. A quotation will serve my need:

"Some years ago," says Mr. Macran, in his introduction to his edition of *Aristoxenus*, "Sir Robert Stewart delivered a lecture in Trinity College, Dublin, on the 'Music of Distant Times and Places,' and included an ancient Greek hymn in his illustrations. It was the unanimous verdict of all the musicians present, that while the music of the less civilised nations was often crude, barbarous, and monotonous in the highest degree, the Greek hymn stood quite

[1] Article on "Musical Rhythm" in *Encyclopædia Britannica*.

Music and Metre

alone in its absolute lack of meaning and its unredeemed ugliness. . . . This criticism is an absurdity, based on the fallacy that music is a universal language. It is impossible to recover the meaning of the dead music of ancient Greece, and well-nigh impossible to accustom our ears to appreciate its form."

After this we may well ask if it is not time to regard as also irrecoverable the relations between quantity and stress and pitch in ancient languages, and abandon further analysis of their verse as a guide to the study of English prosody.

On the subject of quantitative verse in English, it may be well at once to admit, with the prosodist of the *Quarterly Review* (July 1911), that an exotic joy can be obtained from such—much the same, I would add, as is obtained by the lengthening by note in singing of stressed short syllables. The ear can be trained, as Mr. Stone thought it should be, to delight in such numbers and in the combative effects of stress and quantity. Of course the Southey hexameter:

" 'Twás at that / sóber / hóur when the / líght of / dáy is re- / céding,"

is not quantitative verse at all, but simply substitutes so-called accentual dactyls and the rest for quantitative. This species of verse is familiar to us in the poems of Longfellow. Campion condemns English hexameters wholesale : " The heroical verse which is distinguished by the dactyl hath been oftentimes attempted in our English tongue, but with passing pitiful success; and no wonder, seeing it is an attempt altogether against the nature of our language. For both the concourse of our monosyllables make our verses unapt to slide ; and also, if we examine our polysyllables, we shall find few of them, by reason of their heaviness, willing to serve in place of a dactyl." There are two things wrong in this : first, the " concourse of monosyllables " dictum, or what it implies ; second, the supposition that the classical dactyl was a light and tripping measure. With the latter I deal further down.

That the consonantal nature of the English language prevents smoothness is a common fallacy with writers on this matter. Mr. Stone quotes Dr. Whewell's contradiction of it, but shows how the champion of truth in his argument falls at once into other errors. His example is Gray's line :

"The breezy call of incense-breathing morn."

Dr. Whewell remarks on the smoothness of the syllable *-censbr-*, but goes on to say that it is a short syllable. I may leave the length to Mr. Stone, and demur for my part to the taking of the *br-* of " breathing " as part of the preceding syllable. To my ear there is a distinct, though brief, pause between the words " incense " and " breathing." The first question that should be answered by writers who put the classics and English into comparison, is : Were the

Music and Metre

classics *staccato* languages, as English is, spoken word by word, or were they *legato*, like Irish and Italian, with words running into one another? Coventry Patmore thinks that the monosyllables *a, as, ask, asks, ask'st*, though requiring five degrees of time for their articulation, may have precisely the same temporal value in verse; and goes on to doubt the accuracy of the classical rule: "Syllaba brevis unius est temporis, longa vero, duorum." I do not agree that the five English syllables have precisely the same temporal value in verse. The longest of them may be the unstressed syllable of a foot, and the shortest not impossibly the stressed; but that is quite another matter. And even if it were as he says, it would have nothing to do with the Latin rule or with the observation of Dionysius, that "one short syllable differs from another short, and one long from another long."

From tests to which I have submitted many lines of Latin verse, I have come to the conclusion that the classical rule quoted above was accurately observed. In his fine reply to Matthew Arnold's paper *On Translating Homer*, F. W. Newman states that singing to a tune was essential to keep even Greek or Roman poetry to true time. The poetry of these vocalised languages does keep true time, though tune in our sense they could not have; but I know the value of chant in keeping bounds. Mr. Newman is not in love with the idea of poetry sung to a tune; later he says that if we could hear Homer sing his epic verse to an elegant and simple melody—this being the desirable tune—we should complain after twenty lines of meagreness, sameness, and loss of moral expression. The idea of a tune is quite wrong, and indeed tune is undesirable even if possible. "The most beautiful of anthems, after it has been repeated a hundred times on a hundred successive verses, begins to pall on the ear—how much more would an entire book of Homer, if chanted at one sitting!" The word "chant" is here used in a different sense from mine; but I know that the most pleasing chanting, as I understand it, would not save quantitative verse from being intolerable to us, if dealt in large quantities. Mr. Newman himself had experience of it. He had got a Magyar friend of his to recite to him in his native fashion Hungarian quantitative poems. He soon complained, as he says, "gravely" of the monotony. To his ear it was a hideous monotony, like the strumming of very simple music on a single note. It is surely time to give up the effort to reconcile quantitative and accentual verse. "If Homer, at our request" (I quote again), "instead of singing the verses, read or spoke them, then from the loss of well-marked time, and the ascendancy reassumed by the prose accent (?), we should be as helplessly unable to *hear* any metre in them, as are the modern Greeks."

Nor is there greater hope for efforts to reproduce in

Music and Metre

accentual measures the effect of ancient quantitative measures. To the Greeks and Romans, dactylic metres were weighty and sonorous and regular, in measure like, for instance, the " Gloria " of Mozart's *Twelfth Mass*. In English they are tripping or rushing measures. In Greek and Latin the spondee corresponded to a bar of music filled by two crotchets, the dactyl to a similar bar with a crotchet followed by two quavers. The one belongs, as Mr. Omond observes, to as grave an anthem as the other. In English the so-called accentual iambic foot, duple rising metre, is most grave and solemn:

" The wéight of áll the hópes of hálf the wórld."

Duple falling metre may be as solemn :

" Óh, their Dánte of the dréad Inférno ! "

In the classics the *iamb* and the *trochee*, being feet which divided unevenly, the syllables not balancing, were used in light, pliant, colloquial verse, in measure not unlike, perhaps, the music of Gilbert and Sullivan's " I stole the prince and brought him here " in *The Gondoliers*. The *dactyl* and the *spondee* divided evenly with perfect balance.

Here, then, we may leave the " versing " dear, in theory, to Campion, with a passing acknowledgment, by way of conclusion, that he showed frequently, as in his Canto Secundo, a real feeling for quantity, and that for the rest he is true to his own dictum, that "chiefly by accent is the true value of syllables to be measured"—in English. When he left classical patterns and wrote his "English iambic licenciate," his verse, as Samuel Daniel says, "falleth out to be the plain ancient verse consisting of ten syllables which hath ever been used amongst us, time out of mind."

CHAPTER VIII

ACCENT, QUANTITY, PAUSE, EQUIVALENCE

The cause why verses differing in feet yield the same length of sound is by reason of some rests, which either the necessity of the numbers, or the heaviness of the syllables, do beget. CAMPION.

The first rule that is to be observed is the nature of the accent, which we must ever follow. CAMPION.

IN writing English verse, the poet first makes, so to speak, the mould of the verse—or something makes it for him, for *ut poeta, poema nascitur non fit;* something very often that he does not perceive or understand; something—an air of music, a noise in the street, a chance word, a memory, a whim; something or anything. Whatever the nature of the birth or the making, the mould is made. In general the first line shows its form, and following lines conform, though there may be wide scope for variety. It usually happens that a single line of English verse, detached from its context, bears still its mould on its back. But this is not always the case. Finding the mould in the context is sometimes beauty trove, sometimes the finding of disappointment. In a review of

Thomas Campion and the Art of English Poetry

John Davidson's book, *Holiday*, I had read, some years ago, the two lines—

> " From the forest I come whereabout
> The silences, harvested, throng—"

and had found in them a rare beauty of contrast—in the first line a colloquial absence of strong rhythmic stress, in the second the full beat of rich verse rhythm :

> " From the fórest / Í / cóme / whéreabout
> The sílences, hárvested, thróng—"

The context, when I found it, told me that the contrast existed only in my imagination, invented by my reading of it; that the rhythm was just the ordinary so-called anapaestic, triple rising metre :

> " From the fór / est I cóme / whereabóut
> The síl / ences hár / vested thróng—."

Mr. Omond gives a more obvious example, " How happy could I be with either," which fits into either of two moulds, according as the " I " is stressed, or the " be." Sometimes the form does not emerge in full for some lines. The *Quarterly Review* prosodist (July 1911) writes well on this point, but errs extraordinarily in his reading of his example. He quotes Tennyson's well-known song from *Maud* :

> " Come into the garden, Maud,
> For the black bat, Night, has flown,
> Come into the garden, Maud,
> I am here at the gate alone ;
> And the woodbine spices are wafted abroad,
> And the musk of the roses blown."

Accent, Quantity, Pause, Equivalence

Taking the last four lines of this stanza, he says that they are of equivalent length, that there is a silent foot at the end of all but the second last! Now if he had gone on to the following stanza, "For a breeze of morning moves," he would have found a sure example of a silent foot in the odd place; all through the poem he would have found pauses instead of unstressed syllables; but neither here nor elsewhere is there such a silent foot in an even place. The song goes in stanzas of six or eight lines. In all the stanzas the lines in the even places are of three feet. In twenty-eight lines in the odd places there are four feet; in the other nine odd place lines there are three. It becomes clear on reading the poem that the mould is four-foot followed by three-foot. Where there are not actually four stressed syllables in one of the odd lines, there is a silent foot.

One is tempted to quote many examples of this use of the silent foot or the silent syllable from the works of the greatest masters of melody, but such quotation would only draw one further and further from that first rule of Campion's, "the nature of the accent."

On the question of pause in lyric measures Mr. Omond has an excellent chapter. His main example is Browning's "Cavalier Song":

"Kéntish Sir / Býng ₄₄ / stóod for his / kíng ₄₄ /
  Bidding the / cróp-headed / párliament / swíng ₄₄ / . . ."

After "Byng" is a pause equal in length to "headed."

Thomas Campion and the Art of English Poetry

When the mould has got working, the poet could afford to take greater licence with pause. It would not be impossible to have a line like this :

" Márch ᴧᴧ / ón ᴧᴧ / tén ᴧᴧ / stróng ᴧᴧ "

for

" Márched them a / lóng ᴧᴧ / fifty score / stróng ᴧᴧ,"

giving the same effect as such filled-up lines as :

" Hánds from the / pásty, nor / bíte take nor / súp Till you're márching a/lóng . . ."

The unit is the time-space, the period, in which are embedded syllables and pauses. Accent marks off the periods from one another. In a falling metre the stress is on the first syllable of the foot, in a rising metre on the last ; and all forms are reducible to these two, the so-called accentual amphibrach and the like being unnecessary.

As there may be silent syllables and silent feet in song-verse, so there may be silent syllables in speech-verse. The mould, the verse structure, makes clear how many syllables are to be expected, how many are normal. There may be less with pauses to make up the measure, or there may be more, some extra syllables of a light hurrying nature, without breaking the mould :

" Blow, winds, and crack your cheeks ! ᴧ Rage ! ᴧ Blow ! "

" Ò Jóy ! thè Spríng ìs gréen—òn mánỳ à wáll (11 syllables).
  Thè rósès stŕagglè, òn mánỳ à trée dèw-ládèn " (13 syllables)

Accent, Quantity, Pause, Equivalence

In speech-verse the normal line has a fixed number of syllables. In song-verse the normal line has a fixed number of periods, marked by accentual beat, with fixed places for the beat to fall. Of course lyric poems may be composed in lines of different lengths; and there are composite poems, with lines or passages of speech-verse and lines or passages of song-verse, like Wordsworth's great " Ode." Campion has a beautiful poem in the *Observations*, built of alternate lines of speech- and song-verse :

" Constant to none, but ever false to me,
    Traitor still to love through thy faint desires . . ."

These composite poems do not affect the principles of the division into two species.

When a line has less than the normal number of strongly accented syllables, though yet fully syllabled, it will generally be found that secondary stresses enable the mind to hold the norm. So in Campion's line—

" Sómetimes of the póor the rích may bórrow,"

there is a secondary stress on " of."

This matter is not worth dwelling on, but there is another form of verse in which secondary accent plays a larger part. In lines like Campion's :

" And tell the ravisher of my soul I perish for her love,"

it would quite spoil the music of the verse to read with strong accents on the stressed syllables. The verse music is preserved by reading the line like a line of French verse. The tendency of French verse is to feet of one syllable, equal in stress and length. This does not mean that all the stresses and lengths are absolutely equal, but the tendency makes the metrical law.[1] The line from Campion which I have quoted conforms rather to this law than to the English law of strongly-marked accents. It is the presence of such lines in his poetry, introduced into songs of flowing and even stresses, giving a strange pause to too easy and obvious a melody, that made Campion seem so curious a metrist to many. Recently several poets have rediscovered the grace or borrowed it directly from Irish or French. Ernest Dowson's well-known poem, "Non sum qualis eram bonæ sub Regno Cynaræ," explained in an offhand manner, and explained wrongly, by Mr. George Saintsbury in his *Manual of English Prosody*, has this level accent of the straight voice in its lines :

> " I have forgot much, Cynara, gone with the wind,
> Flung roses, roses, riotously with the throng,
> Dancing, to put thy pale lost lilies out of mind,
> But I was desolate and sick of an old passion—
>   Yea, all the time, because the dance was long.
> I have been faithful to thee, Cynara, in my fashion."

This may be read—not without wrenching and difficulty—according to Mr. Saintsbury's "scansion" of it :
" I have / been faith / ful to / thee, Cy / nara, in / my fashion,"
but so read it loses all its distinction.

[1] See *Quarterly Review*, July 1911.

Accent, Quantity, Pause, Equivalence

My next example shows a line of this kind followed by one of sounding rhythm :

" When I am gone and you alone are living here still
You'll thínk / of mé / when spléndid // the stórm / is ón / the híll."

In this I think that the prose rhythm of the first line accentuates the verse rhythm of the second.

It will be noticed that in these examples the lines are always long. In short lines the ear counts and arranges. Ordinarily lines of English verse (song and speech) are of not more than five feet, or length corresponding to five feet. Campion shrewdly remarked that English will not bear long lines in verse. He held that the English heroic line is equal in time-length to the Latin hexameter. Lines of greater length are generally broken by a cesural pause after the third or fourth foot :

" Then burst with sighing in her sight // and ne'er return again."

Of course it is possible to manufacture lines with dissyllabic or polysyllabic words crossing the cesural joints ; but it is also possible to manufacture lines in which the endings are crossed in the same way :

" . . . For fear of that, I still
Will stay with thee, and never from this palace of dim night depart again—here, here
Will I remain with worms that are thy chamber-maids. . . ."

This is a passage from *Romeo and Juliet* reset. It is possible at all times to perform *tours de force*. They must be recognised as such. "The ear is," as Campion says, "a rational sense, and a chief judge of proportion." The ear has declared lines of one syllable and of one hundred syllables, of one foot or of twenty-one, against the law. There must then be zones. A single line of one syllable among longer lines is possible, and is occasionally found, mostly in the Caroline poets and in Francis Thompson. Single lines of two syllables are more common. Two consecutive lines of one syllable, or two of two syllables, would coalesce, and, however printed, would form one line of two or one line of four syllables.[1] Poems of three-syllable lines, with two accents, are common enough; they have generally a burlesque effect:

> "Little boy,
> Pair of skates:
> Broken ice,
> Heaven's gates."

On the contrary, lines of four syllables, two stresses, may be dignified and serious, like Campion's "Anacreontic":

> "Time can conquer
> Love's unkindness;
> Love can alter
> Time's disgraces."

---

[1] It would seem that there should be in a line syllables enough to make a rhythm, and that two syllables are not enough; but Herrick's poem, "Upon his departure hence," gives one pause.

Accent, Quantity, Pause, Equivalence

As I believe the longest true line, indivisible, of English verse to be of five feet, and as not more than three syllables ordinarily go to a foot, the major zone I should fix at fifteen syllables, with stressed ending, or sixteen, with unstressed. Seventeen, with double stressed, would be possible.

So much for length of line by number of syllables and by number of feet founded on accent. I have just said that as a general rule not more than three syllables go to a foot. This is by no means an arbitrary limitation. A foot, of one stressed, or of one stressed and one or more unstressed, is produced by one effort or pressure of the voice.[1] The word " tremendous " is one pressure, " intervene " is two. Mr. Omond claims that words like " memorial " and " superfluous " are four-syllable monopressures, while at the same time stating that very many monopressures can be rattled off in one breath by fluent speakers. But if rattling off in one breath be put aside, then " memorial " and " superfluous " have two monopressures each. My conclusion is that, rattled off in a certain way, there may be feet of more than three syllables ; if, then, the law of monopressures govern the foot, there may be more than three syllables in a monopressure. Some time ago I took a note of a very vigorous piece of talk which I heard from an

[1] This law was first stated in a book published anonymously in 1888, *Accent and Rhythm explained by the Law of Monopressure*. The law has been adopted and amplified by Professor Skeat.

old woman in Co. Tipperary. Her house had been honoured one Sunday morning by a visit from the local county councillor, who came to invite her son, a labourer, to join the boys of the village, shopkeepers and farmers' sons, on an excursion to the neighbouring village of Toomeyvara.

" Get up, says he,[1] / quick, says he / out of that, says he, / says Paddy Molloy, says he, / to my Patsy, says he. /

" He will, says I, / and what's more, says I, / he'll have a shilling in his pocket, says I, / to spend with the rest of the boys, says I. /

" Doesn't matter about that, says he, / but the boys are waiting in the brake, says he, / and they'll be late for second mass in Toomeyvara, says he, /

" If he doesn't get up, says he, / quick, says he, / out of that, says he. / "

In this there was a *crescendo* and a *decrescendo*, increasing with the excitement of the narrative, and then dying away before the finality of the repetition. The old woman had told the story to many in the same way before I heard it. It had assumed a kind of metrical form; and in it, I believe, we have an example of verse in process of evolution.

However Professor Skeat may err in fixing three syllables as the limit of the monopressure, or Mr. Omond in hearing only one monopressure in "superfluous," I believe that they are right in their main theory. It is certain that there cannot be feet of very

---

[1] The word " says " all through is a mere hiss.

Accent, Quantity, Pause, Equivalence

many syllables ; certain also, I think, that the number of syllables in a foot is governed by voice pressure. The main accent falls on one syllable of the monopressure, and therefore of the foot. In words of more than one syllable there is a rule of pronunciation which fixes on which syllable this accent falls. When a foot is composed of monosyllables, the strength of accent on a certain syllable depends on the sense and the nature of the surrounding syllables.[1] The prose sentence, " I come from Cork," may be accented in four different ways. So it will be seen that in accented verse, the foot, marked by the accent, really depends on the line, or on the larger unit, the paragraph. In quantitative verse all is different. The line depends on the feet, and the feet on the syllables of the words, of which the quantity is fixed.

In English also the quantity is fixed, inherent in the words, but it does not govern scansion, and has not a directive force in the making of verse. There are, it is generally stated, two ways in which a syllable may be long—in its vowel, and in its vowel and consonants. " Go " is long. The " o " of " frost " is short, but the syllable is considered long. There are in English degrees of length. Coventry Patmore's five syllables, " a, as, ask, asks, ask'st," will serve to show differences, and serve also to show the impossibility of laying down any rule or coming to any con-

[1] Account must also be taken of the inter-word pause in English.

clusion in such cases. As a matter of fact the length of " go " and the length, or rather slowness, of " asks " are two different things. " Go " is long. Is " ghosts," then, to be treated as ultra-long, or what ? If " a- " before " -sks " is long by position, as Campion would have it—that is, if the syllable is long, though the vowel short—then either quantity must be quite neglected in treating of the rules of verse in English, or we must go back and reconsider the theories of Campion and all who held that a syllable may be lengthened by consonants in English as in Latin.

I believe that I have discovered the true explanation, and the cause of difference in this matter between the classics and English, in the fact that the classics, more highly vocalised as they were, were *legato* languages, like Irish and Italian, without the English " rests or natural breathing-places " between the words ; while English is a *staccato* language, with such rests. Mr. Stone, in disallowing elision in English verse (rightly, I think), says that Milton's use of it is a fiction. I do not think so. Rather I think that the language may formerly have been *legato-staccato*, or at least had a *legato* tendency in verse, but is now definitely *staccato*. I propose that in considering quantity in English, account be taken only of the vowel, leaving the inter-word rest to overcome the length or difficulty of the consonants—to vocalise, as it were. In their references to consonant length all

Accent, Quantity, Pause, Equivalence

writers on this matter are vague, from Campion, who found that " the concourse of our monosyllables make our verses unapt to slide," to Dr. Whewell with his syllable " -censbr- " from " incense-breathing." It may be said that taking account of the inter-word pause will rather lengthen the syllable with many consonants. As a matter of fact, in speaking English, as in reading English verse, we do take account of it. My contention is that so-called long syllables, made slow by glut of consonants, should be considered in connection with *pause*, not with *quantity ;* that the syllable " ghosts " is long, and the syllable " gusts " is short ; that a long syllable has a long vowel, and a short, a short vowel. Example is the best definition. Mr. Omond quotes as an offensive line :

" 'Twas thou that smooth'd'st the rough rugg'd bed of pain."

The difficulties here are phonetic. In " smooth'd'st " it is hard to mark the transition from " th " to " d," from spirant to voiced dental, without intermediate vowel. It is still harder to make the " d " heard between " th " and " st." In order to make an approach to full pronunciation, one has to go slowly. The word " smooth'd'st " is difficult and offensive in prose or verse ; indeed, it would scarcely be allowed in prose. The combination " rough rugg'd " presents similar obstacles to smooth reading.

The slowness of such a line as this may be

a fault, but, as Pope knew, it may be used with effect :

> " When Ajax strives some rock's vast weight to throw,
> The line too labours, and the words move slow."

To be considered under the heading of Quantity remain long-vowel and short-vowel syllables. Every simple vowel in English may be long or short. The simple vowels, front and back—in Irish, slender and broad—are, from the highest to the lowest, "i, e, a (man), a (all), o, u."

	i, short in	" ill,"	long in	" eel " ;
	e, ,,	" ell,"	,,	" ale " ;
front a,	,,	" man,"	,,	" mar " (approximately, as pronounced in Ireland) ;
back a,	,,	" doll,"	,,	" all " ;
	o, ,,	" ton,"	,,	" tone " ;
	u, ,,	" full,"	,,	" fool."

Of course English spelling, as in " ale " and " doll," should not prevent us from considering these words under the vowel sounds found in them—" e," and " a " back. Vowels like the " i " of " white," not simple, are always long. All the vowels of a line of English verse may be long, or all may be short, but almost always there is a combination of long and short vowels. The stress may fall on the long or on the short. When it falls on a short, it lingers, giving to the short vowel a certain quality of slowness—*cf.* :

> " Thĕ sĕcŭlár ăbўss tŏ cómĕ."

Accent, Quantity, Pause, Equivalence

When the unstressed vowels are all short, and the stressed all long, the result is the smoothness of regular movement—*cf.* Tennyson's

"Thĕ vóice ŏf dáys ŏf óld ănd dáys tŏ bé,
Whén áll ŏf hígh ănd hólў díes ăwáy."

When all the vowels, or a large number of them, stressed and unstressed, are long, the result is an effect of slowness, at times even of motionlessness. Mr. Russell (" Æ "), of whom I have written above, has quoted to me lines in which he tried to produce the effect of the placidity of a lake, and we remarked that the vowels were mostly long.

The lines quoted in this connection by the *Quarterly Review* writer (July 1911) will serve to link this division of my subject, Quantity, with the next, Equivalence.

"Slēēp ōn / mў̄ lōve / ĭn thȳ / cōld bēd,
Nēvĕr / tŏ bē̆ / dīsquī / ĕtĕd." [1]

"The discrepancy "—I quote—" between the lines is a delight to the ear, which preserves a reconciling unity. And the secret of the reconciliation is equivalence or substitution."

Equivalence Mr. Saintsbury defines as " the quality or faculty which fits one combination of syllables for substitution in the place of another to perform the part of foot, as the dactyl and spondee do to each other in the classical hexameter." But he warns us

[1] The quantity marks are not mine.

Thomas Campion and the Art of English Poetry

that substitution "must not take place in a batch of lines, or even (with rare exceptions) in a single line, to such an extent that the base of the metre can be mistaken." With this limitation, it may be said that every foot in English is equal to every other foot. An example of the violation of the base or norm of the metre appears in a poem by the Honourable Emily Lawless, published in *The Irish Review*. The base is triple rising four-stress, but there is free use of equivalence, with lines like:

"Jíngling and jángling down Árdaneer shóre,"

so that when a stanza begins with

"Easy, Morough, said I, don't waste your blows,"

one easily reads

"Eásy / Mórough / said Í / don't wáste / ——,"

instead of

"Easy Mór/ough, said I, / don't wáste / your blóws."

It will be seen that the line would read as well if "easy" or "Morough" or "said I" were omitted.

Campion, who seems to have discovered equivalence for himself, lays down definite rules and limits for its use—for instance, that it must not take place in the third or fifth foot of a pentameter line with rising stresses. This is not strict, and at all events the ear, that "rational sense," and not the thumb, is chief judge.

Accent, Quantity, Pause, Equivalence

I close this chapter with a few examples of the use of equivalence, which will tell more of this quality or faculty of verse than all my prosing :

(1) " Lóok to / the blów / ing róse / abóut / us—' Ló,
　　Laúghing,' / she sáys, / ' ínto / the wórld / I blów.' "
(2) " Laúgheth / at hím, / mócked by / vísions / of góld."

In these the norm is five-stress duple rising metre. In the following example the first line shows the norm :

(3) " Is it / so small / a thing
　　To have / enjoyed / the sun
　　To have lív'd / líght / in the spríng,
　　To have lóv'd, / to have thóught, / to have done ;
To have advanced true friends and beat down baffling foes ? "

CHAPTER IX

RIME

*Non satis est pulchra esse poemata, dulcia sunto
Et quocumque volent animum auditoris agunto.*

HORACE.

We are like to have lean numbers instead of fat rime.
SAMUEL DANIEL.

IT is in connection with rime, and with the old contention concerning the use of rime, that Campion's *Observations* is commonly remembered. There are, of course, good reasons for this, yet, on coming to examine the matter, one finds that this question of all he has treated in the most cursory manner—in prose only some vague generalities and indictments; in verse, lyrics carefully unrimed, but at their best saved by chiming assonances. And then, after Daniel's *Defence*, no other word from Campion against the "fatness of rime," or its shiftiness or flattery or ease, but always lyrics graced with pealing and carolling returns of like sounds. Of course, in this as in his treatment of quantity, Campion was led astray by his false notions of classic verse. As a matter of fact, quantitative verse, as quantitative verse, could not well rime. The Leonine hexameter, though it can be scanned quantitatively, must be read as accentual verse if the rime is to be heard:

"Post cœnam stabis : seu passus mille meabis."

Here " sta- " is the last syllable of one foot, and " -bis " the first of another foot, while the " -abis " of " meabis " is a foot of itself. The same is generally true of the so-called riming lines of Horace and Ovid:

"Ille gravem du<u>ro</u> terram qui vertit arat<u>ro</u>." (Horace.)
"Quot cœlum stell<u>as</u> tot habet tua Roma puell<u>as</u>." (Ovid.)[1]

And, indeed, if the similar syllables both occurred at the end of a foot, they would still make no rime, as the feet, in the hexameter, all correspond to accentual falling stresses, and would call for double or triple rime. The only possible rime that I can remember in the classics is double; it occurs in Horace's *Ars Poetica*, and has served me as a motto for this chapter—appropriately, I think, for the sweetness added to beauty by other graces in the classic tongues is best attained in English verse by rime.

Rime, then, has no place in quantitative verse. Rime, I hold, evolves naturally in accentual verse, more especially in accentual song-verse. It is, I believe, quite idle to claim for the Irish or the Persians or others the glory of having invented rime for all the riming world, of having introduced it into this foreign

[1] Quoted by Campion.

tongue or that. The languages invented it. When the stress of accentual verse falls on vowel after vowel, assonance is sure to catch the ear, and from assonance to rime is but a step—and a step sure to be taken by a language with the phonetic physique of English. The late William Larminie, in an interesting though faulty paper in the *Contemporary Review* (November 1894), drew attention to the use of assonance in Homer, and claimed that the verse of the *Odyssey* was poorer than that of the *Iliad* for want of that grace. Mr. A. C. Bradley, writing on the impossibility of expressing in translation what has been greatly and duly said, instances Virgil's line :

" Tendebantque manus ripæ ulterioris amore."

" If I translate this," he says, " ' and were stretching forth their hands in longing for the further bank,' the charm of the original has fled. . . . Because I have changed the *meaning* of Virgil's line. What that meaning is *I* cannot say. Virgil has said it. But I can see this much, that the translation conveys a far less vivid picture of the outstretched hands and of their remaining outstretched, and a far less poignant sense of the distance of the shore and the longing of the souls. And it does so partly because this picture and this sense are conveyed not only by the obvious meaning of the words, but through the long-drawn sound of ' tendebant manus,' through the time occu-

Rime

pied by the five syllables, and therefore by the idea of 'ulterioris,' and through the identity of the long sound 'or' in the penultimate syllables of 'ulterioris amore '—all this and much more, apprehended not in this analytical fashion, nor as *added* to the beauty of mere sound and to the obvious meaning, but in unity with them and so as expressive of the poetic meaning of the whole."

I have quoted this in full, as it introduces for me other things which I wish to join here to my analysis of rime. That Virgil was conscious of the assonance in that line, and elsewhere in his work, is as certain as that Milton was aware of the assonance in the famous passage cited by Mr. Larminie:

" Thus with the years
Seasons return, but not to me returns
Day or the sweet approach of ev'n or morn. . . ."

Mr. Larminie did not go on to say that this showed assonance to be a grace of both rimed and unrimed verse, which should not, in English, take the place of rime. On the contrary, he essayed himself to reproduce in English some of the assonantal measures of Irish. He too, like those who confuse quantity with accent, failed to perceive an essential difference. Irish is a highly vocalised language, with abundance of open vowels, and English such that in it assonance can go only a little way, where rime can go far. His own experiments fall into rime very soon.

Assonance is really of two kinds, or, perhaps it should be said, has two uses. With assonance of one kind all the most musical English verse is saturated; this is what may be called vowel alliteration. The other kind, as in Mr. Larminie's verses, is simply a kind of end-rime in which only the vowel sound is repeated, the consonants differing:

> " Let him seek the southern hills
> And those lakes of loveliest water
> Where the richest bloom of spring's
> Burns to reddest autumn."
>
> *Fand and Other Poems.*

An ancient Gaelic poet would have burned to reddest anger at some of Larminie's assonances. In Irish the thing was, as Professor Atkinson said, "not imperfect rime, but something far richer than rime, and admitting of a far more complex series of harmonies." The broad vowels, " a, o, u," the slender, " e, i," were allowed to assonate only with members of their own classes; and the diphthongs were similarly divided according to predominating broads and slenders. Nor was this all. Every consonant was limited to assonance with members of its own class. The classes: the soft, " c, p, t "; the hard, " b, g, d "; the rough, " ch, ph, th, sh "; the strong, " ll, nn, rr, m, ng "; the light, " v, gh, dh, l, n, r "; the one weak consonant, " f "; the one barren, " s." It will be seen that these are divided on phonetic principles; one may be assured

Rime

that the Irish rules of assonance were at first a record of custom evolved through the nature of the language. Owing to the signs of skill and scholarship in poetry and prosody in ancient Ireland, some apologists have claimed that thence has come all that is good in the poetry and prosody of such modern languages as English, through Latin Celticised by the Irish monks and by Celts of the Continent. Dr. Kuno Meyer is not one of these. " The original type," he says, "from which the great variety of Irish metres has sprung, is the catalectic trochaic tetrameter of Latin poetry, as in the well-known popular song of Cæsar's soldiers :

"Cæsar Gallias subegit,   Nicomedes Cæsarem,
Ecce Cæsar nunc triumphat   qui subegit Gallias."

On the other hand, Dr. Sigerson, in the introduction to his fine book, *Bards of the Gael and Gaul*, holds that the earliest Latin poetry was of Gaelic form, and, I think, makes good his case, as when he shows that Cicero's lines read well if taken as conforming to the rules of Old Irish verse :

" Cedant arma togæ   concedat laurea linguæ,
O fortunatam natam   me consule Romam."

But when all this is said, when all is proved and admitted, even taking into account the obvious and inevitable influence of imitation in such an imitative art as poetry, it remains certain, I think, that an accentual language like English, having come into existence, would of itself have evolved into a riming-verse language. And indeed, did not Anglo-Saxon show an inclination to rime in Cynewulf, in Caedmon, in the *Beowulf?*

The French writer Guyau, in his *Problèmes de l'Esthétique Contemporaine*, analyses rime specifically : " It is well known that in language each vowel has a particular *timbre*, which is nothing more than the chord formed by its fundamental note and the elemental sounds called harmonics or over-tones. All language is therefore a succession of chords, but in prose they succeed one another irregularly, in verse they recur in equal numbers and at equal intervals. . . . Rime completes the harmony by the chords on which the rhythmical cadence rests ; this regular echo, by itself, is not lacking in charm. But further, since each vowel has its own *timbre*, the rimed vowels will have something of the varied *timbre* of instruments ; some, like long ' a ' (in French), resemble the double-bass ; others, like ' i,' have the acuteness of the clarinet or the flute ; each verse can be recognised by the quality of its final syllable ; some, so to speak, are accompanied by one instrument, others by another, and we experience a pleasure, as we perceive the different qualities in the stanza, similar to that of the musician as he distinguishes the different instruments in the orchestra taking up one after another a melodic phrase."

Rime

This is interesting, though not calculated really to lead one further towards truth in the matter. It resembles in some details the extraordinary " Note on Poetry " affixed by John Davidson to his *Holiday and Other Poems*, which begins by marking rime as a property of decadence, and goes on to terms of cymbals and oboes, tabors and clarigolds, psalteries and sackbuts and timbrels. But both these writers have perceived the value of contrast in rime, one of its most musical properties. My next illustration is an experiment which shows such contrast of end-rimes enhanced by monotony of internal rime and assonance :

" Now noon is far, the dusk more narrow grows ;
 And soon a star will hush the sparrows' din,
 And fold them all the stooping eaves within ;
 Then cold will fall with drooping leaves the rose,
 The lilac flow'rs will drink the dew and close ;
 And silent hours will link anew and spin
 The world and thought round seasons of repose."

The last line stands relieved of the heavy internal rimes.

For myself, I feel that in English song-verse gives rime in answer to the call of music. Lyric measures sing themselves into verse in a poet's brain. I cannot imagine one writing unrimed verse to the tune of " Home, sweet Home."

Having come, rime was promptly turned to use

Thomas Campion and the Art of English Poetry

The earliest writers claim it as an aid to memory and the like. Such things are neither here nor there. Similarly, Campion bewails the fact that rime is easy, and "creates as many poets as a hot summer flies"—as if the doggerel of such were a reason or an argument. The worthy use of rime is different from that which sets a glory to a tale of kings in a child's history book. Rime is, in the first place, replete with emotion, and emotion is the spring of poetry. And then, as Samuel Daniel finely said, rime "gives wings to the poet to mount, and carries him not out of his course, but, as it were, beyond his power to a far happier flight." But the poet of whom he speaks is "an eminent spirit whom nature hath fitted for that mystery," not one who can, as Campion said, be enforced by rime "to abjure his matter and extend a short conceit beyond all bounds of art." John Davidson speaks of the "wasteful and ridiculous excess" to which rime led Shakespeare in his best sonnets, in the famous seventy-third:

> "That time of year thou may'st in me behold
> When yellow leaves, or none, or few, do hang
> Upon those boughs which shake against the cold—
> Bare ruined choirs where late the sweet birds sang."

It is the rime, he thinks, that requires "or none, or few," the rime that gives "those boughs which shake against the cold," and then those "bare ruined choirs."

Rime

One needs no further comment. He goes on to contrast these lines with Macbeth's

> " My way of life
> Is fallen into the sere, the yellow leaf,"

and says it makes one feel that there is a great gulf fixed between rime and blank verse. It is not essentially a matter of rime and non-rime, but of song-verse and speech-verse.

Rime is found in both. In speech-verse poems such as the sonnet, in poems in heroic couplets and in stanzas of one kind or another, when, in addition to the balance of the verse-weight, there is also the balance of the parts, octave and sestet, couplet and couplet, stanza and stanza, and the necessity of rounding off the parts, rime is used to bind and to contrast.

In some well-known speech-verse poems, such as Browning's *Sordello*, the rime is a vain elegance. On the other hand, the rime of Keats' *Endymion* has a melody of its own, as of a more beautiful speech. Such a use of rime might justify its presence always in speech-verse, making us half forget Milton's grave blank verse, if we had not *Hyperion* to show again that this form at its greatest dispenses with such ornament.

In song-verse rime is so obviously a component that the exceptional unrimed lyric is more interesting—

such a poem as Collins's "Ode to Evening" or Campion's "Rose-cheek'd Laura."[1] In both, assonance and the ringing of all the changes of vowel sounds make the absence of end-rime a delight.

> "If aught of oaten stop, or pastoral song,
>   May hope, chaste Eve, to soothe thy modest ear,
>   Like thy own solemn springs,
>   Thy springs and dying gales."

> "Rose-cheek'd Laura, come;
>   Sing thou smoothly with thy beauty's
>   Silent music, either other
>   Sweetly gracing;
>   Lovely forms do flow
>   From content divinely framed;
>   Heav'n is music, and thy beauty's
>   Birth is heavenly.
>   These dull notes we sing
>   Discords need for helps to grace them,
>   Only beauty purely loving
>   Knows no discord,
>   But still moves delight,
>   Like clear springs renew'd by flowing,
>   Ever perfect, ever in themselves eternal."

Such poems legitimately dispense with rime, and show us the way to a new song-verse—not William Larminie's way. And yet it seems that something of what Larminie looked for is to come. In recent Anglo-Irish poems there is a growing use of a form

[1] Given in the *Observations* as an example of the ditty or ode.

Rime

in which the traditional English end-rime is heightened by internal assonance. The following is from a version of a Gaelic poem:

> "But sweeter than violin or lute
> Is my love, and she left me behind;
> I wish that all music were mute
> And I to all beauty were blind."

In this will be seen another necessary characteristic of both Gaelic and Anglo-Saxon verse, alliteration—and used to emphasize the assonating syllables. And, economically to make the one example serve as instance of many things, in this will be seen the difference between assonance (which can use a final syllable or monosyllable, as "mute," to chime with any syllable of a word, as "beauty") and rime (which demands for its vowel in both riming words the same position).

In his *Apologie for Poetrie*, Sir Philip Sidney claimed that English is fortunate in its rimes, having single, double, and triple rime-endings, whereas French has only single and double. The advantage is small—in modern English, at least—for Sidney's examples, "motion," "potion," are no longer triple, and those that preserve that character are frequently burlesque. Indeed, Sidney's claim only draws attention to a real poverty in one section.

The Irish language, which is full of such triple endings, has a wealth of all that makes for resonant rich music,

Thomas Campion and the Art of English Poetry

but shows, I believe, that such wealth is in reality a lure, and might with justice receive the blame which Campion showered on English rime, that it makes verse too easy. On the other hand, in English many versifiers fall into a round of common rimes, which soon pall on the ear. One of the worst examples of this fault is the much-famed work of a true poet, Oliver Goldsmith's *The Traveller*. In the twenty lines beginning " To men of other minds my fancy flies," the rimes are : " flies, lies ; stand, land ; tide, pride ; slow, grow ; roar, shore ; pile, smile ; vale, sail ; plain, reign." And this is not the most monotonous passage. Further down there are eight assonances to " train " in ten lines. If there were an effect of onomatopœia in this monotony, there would be virtue in it ; but in *The Traveller* there is only vice, and that worst of vices, poverty.

It is not necessary to speak of the hideous rimes of Mrs. Browning, or of the occasional far-fetched juggling of the great poet, her husband. It is a more gracious task to seek virtue in the fine, careless rapture of the incorrect rimes of some exquisite lyric poets. First instance, Shelley's " Skylark " :

> " Hail to thee, blithe spirit !
> Bird thou never wert—
> That from heaven or near it
> Pourest thy full heart
> In profuse strains of unpremeditated art."

Rime

All through the poem there is this same winging upwards to right and left, as it were, instead of striking straight in accurate rime. The ecstasy of the poem goes with the winging; whereas, in a contemplative ode like Keats' "Grecian Urn," the "priest" and "drest," ending the second and fourth lines of a stanza, really leave these lines blank. And there is still another aspect of the thing. Once a grace, this carelessness of rime was sure to become an artifice. Many of Mr. Yeats' recent poems seem to be careful in their avoidance of correct rime. But for all that the thing may yet be a grace, something like the blank line in *Omar*, left hanging in the air, or the blank line in Campion's "Hark, all you ladies." Even more, it may be a refusal, something that does not bend to an obvious chime :

> " So, harsh and bare, your bitter heart
>   Will leave you like a bush alone,
> Sullen and silent and apart,
>   When all the winds it called are gone—
> The winds were airs of your own heart ! "

It would have been so easy to write :

> " When all the winds it called have blown."

Rime, I have said, demands for its vowel the same position in both riming words. When a dissyllable or polysyllable is accented on the last, as "release" or "wandering," with primary or secondary accent, there is nothing peculiar in their riming with a monosyllable. When, however, as in "lady," the prose accent throws the stress on the first syllable, there is a quaintness in riming the word with a monosyllable. In Old Irish, which was syllabic, one of the most important verse forms, the *debide* (*dhevee*), was hepta-syllabic, with the second line of each couplet ending in a word one syllable longer than the end word of the first line, with which it assonated or rimed :

> " Messe ocus Pangur bān,
> Cechtar nathar fria saindan."

Campion's first published poem, " Hark, all you ladies," to which I have so often to refer, has rimes like this :

> " In myrtle arbours on the downs
>   The fairy-queen Proserpina,
> This night by moonshine leading merry rounds,
>   Holds a watch with sweet love,
>   Down the dale, up the hill ;
>   No plaints or groans may move
>   Their holy vigil."

Another most lovely poem will serve as an example both of this and of Campion's use of internal rime :

> " What then is love but mourning ?
>   What desire, but a self-burning ?
>   Till she, that hates, doth love return,
>   Thus will I mourn, thus will I sing,
>   ' Come away ! come away, my darling ! '

Rime

Beauty is but a blooming,
Youth in his glory entombing;
Time hath a while, which none can <u>stay</u>;
Then come <u>away</u>, while thus I <u>sing</u>,
' Come <u>away</u>! come away, my <u>darling</u>!'

Summer in winter fadeth;
Gloomy night heavenly light shadeth:
Like to the morn are Venus' <u>flow'rs</u>;
Such are her <u>hours</u>: then will I <u>sing</u>,
' Come <u>away</u>! come away, my <u>darling</u>!'"

Mr. Percival Vivian suspects that this riming of "vigil" and "darling" with "hill" and "sing" "is in some way due to the effect of musical accent." With Campion music is never far off, but phonetics suffice here. Unstressed syllables riming with stressed syllables will be found to be of the same pitch. Words like "lady," "beauty," "darling," "vigil," which are found in such rimes, all end in a front vowel. All these words rise in their last syllable to the pitch of the monosyllable with which they rime. "Beauty" is a good example. "U" is the deepest back vowel, the "wu, wu" of the mastiff; and "i" (English "ee") the high front vowel, the "wi, wi" of the smallest puppy.

It may be asked if, after what I have written in a previous chapter of dividing lines of long verse into short lines, there can be, according to my system, such a thing as internal rime—if the rime does not automatically break up the line. It does not. Internal rimes will be found to be less emphatic than end-rimes, as can be seen in Tennyson's

> " The splendour falls on castle walls,
>   And snowy summits old in story ;
> The long light shakes across the lakes,
>   And the wild cataract leaps in glory,"

or in the example from Campion given above.

Such internal rimes will most frequently be found in verse arranged in stanzas. Indeed, I think that the stanza form may have been a powerful factor in the development of rime in late Latin and in the languages influenced by it. The stanzas of the classic poets, who eschewed all grace of repetition, could not, of course, have suggested rime, but at an early stage appeared the device of repeating a refrain. John Davidson sees in the use of re-echoing rime—a word riming to itself—a new order evolving from new decay. It has come from America, he says—from America, which is the decadence of Europe. He glories in the decadence, and rhapsodises on the intensity of the mood in which Edgar Allan Poe discovered that a word can rime to itself with an entirely new sound, if the preceding phraseology be changed. For my part, I think that this re-echo rather preceded rime as we know it, and not improbably suggested it, even before stress-rhythm made it inevitable ; so that in this, as in all such, Plato the divine and Solomon may be justified in their sentences, that all knowledge is but recollection, and all novelty but oblivion.

Davidson's treatment of the matter is at once exaggerated and incomplete. It is true that a word may rime to itself with a new sound, and possibly with more music than a new word. This is perhaps due to the unexpectedness of the repetition in our rime-trained ears, and also to the reassertion, as it were, contained in the return to the same chord. A stanza quoted above ("So, harsh and bare") will serve as an example.

This re-echo preceded rime. The refrains of Theocritus, Catullus, and Virgil could not, in quantitative verse, have developed towards rime ; but when word-accent came in and stressed certain syllables of the verse, when these syllables began more and more to coincide with the first of the feet, it needed only a frequently recurring refrain to join and lead the way. The *Pervigilium Veneris* has both stress and refrain :

" Cras amet qui nunquam amavit, quique amavit cras amet.
  ver novum, ver iam canorum, ver renatus orbis est ;
  vere concordant amores, vere nubunt alites,
  et nemus comam resolvit de maritis imbribus.
  . . . .
  Cras amet qui nunquam amavit, quique amavit cras amet.
  . . . .

Thomas Campion and the Art of English Poetry

> Illa cantat, nos tacemus ; quando ver venit meum ?
> quando fiam uti chelidon vel tacere desinam ?
> perdidi Musam tacendo, nec me Phœbus respicit ;
> sic Amylcas cum tacerent perditit silentium.
> Cras amet qui nunquam amavit, quique amavit cras amet."

Mr. J. W. Mackail has written with something of lyric rapture of this poem. He errs, I think, with W. J. Stone, in attributing word-stress to all Latin verse, and in finding frequent accidental rimes in Latin, but for the rest is suggestive and incisive. With the revival of the trochaic movement, which had been freely used by the earliest Latin poets, he holds that we are on the very verge of the accentual Latin poetry of the Middle Ages. The affinity is made closer by the free use of initial and terminal assonances.

And now I have come to the end of my survey of the Art of English Poetry, founded on Campion's *Observations*. I had intended to add a chapter on the few signs that I have discovered of Campion's influence, and on some of his original metres. I have, however, little sympathy with those who find an influence in every similarity, however obvious and general the thought and expression. I think worthy of mention only two such parallels. All that I had to say of metres I have embodied in previous chapters

Rime

and in this. Nothing remains for me to do in this connection but to state that I claim for all prosody a recording function only, never a directive. The prosody of to-day is not as it was in Campion's age; it progresses with the art. The next poet may extend the dominion, and call the metrists in his wake.

My first parallel is between Campion and William Blake—between Campion's "When the god of merry love," in *A Book of Airs*, and Blake's "Mental Traveller" and other poems; between Campion's poem on "Human Pity" and two or three of Blake's. I am aware that these similarities may lead nowhere. I do not wish to prove more than I believe. It would be difficult to prove that Blake ever read Campion or even heard of him; but Blake may very well have differed from his contemporaries in his library of poets as in other things. No poet of his age so nearly catches and repeats the music of the song-books and of Campion; whether from the song-books or not, we shall probably never know.

The other parallel is between Campion and Milton—between Campion's "Jack and Joan they think no ill" and Milton's *L'Allegro*, the passage beginning "Sometimes with secure delight." Here again I do not wish to urge the comparison. Mr. Saintsbury declares that he would give much to know whether Milton had read Campion. It is highly improbable that he could have escaped reading him. The great poet's nephew, Edward Phillips, was acquainted with Campion's work, however little he thought of it.[1] It is more than likely that the young poet-musician of *L'Allegro* knew and appreciated Campion's *Airs*, still more likely that the writer of the famous note, "The Verse," prefixed to *Paradise Lost*, was interested in the rime controversy. Indeed, on the strength of the close likeness between Milton's note and the second chapter of the *Observations*, one might go further. Like Campion, too, Milton recanted, if not in prose declaration, in song. With no more splendid example of its use could I close this chapter on rime than with the final chorus from *Samson Agonistes*, letting Canon H. C. Beeching preach its sermon for me. His text is Milton's declaration that rime is " as a thing of itself trivial and of no musical delight."

" Is the rime of this fine passage otiose and trivial ? No one can fail to observe what variety it lends to the chorus, by ringing the changes on all the chief vowel sounds, or how it marks sections of thought—first the text, then the illustration, then the moral. The second section, indeed, runs on into the third set of rimes, but by that slight irregularity the ode is bound together, and the ear kept on the alert, until the full close, for the rime that is sure to come."

[1] He mentions Camden's reference to Campion in his *Theatrum Poetarum*.

Rime

"All is best, though we oft doubt,
What th' unsearchable dispose
Of highest wisdom brings about,
And ever best found in the close.
Oft he seems to hide his face,
But unexpectedly returns
And to his faithful Champion hath in place
Bore witness gloriously, whence Gaza mourns
And all that band them to resist
His uncontrollable intent.
His servants he with new acquist
Of true experience from this great event
With peace and consolation hath dismist,
And calm of mind all passion spent."

APPENDICES

APPENDIX A

SUMMARY OF KNOWN FACTS RELATING TO THOMAS CAMPION, ARRANGED CHRONOLOGICALLY [1]

1564. John Campion, "son of John Campion of Dublin, Ireland, deceased," married Lucy Trigg, *née* Searle.

1565. Rose Campion, sister of poet, born. John Campion, his father, admitted to Middle Temple.

1566. John Campion a Cursitor of the Chancery Court.

1567. Thomas Campion born. Christened at St. Andrew's Church, Holborn.

1573. "John Campion Gentleman" elected Vestryman of St. Andrew's.

1576. John Campion died. Lucy Campion and her children went to live on their property at Brokenborough, Wilts.

1577. Lucy Campion married her third husband, Augustine Steward, of the family from which Oliver Cromwell was descended through his mother, Elizabeth Steward.

1580. Poet's mother died.

1581. Thomas Campion (*ætat.* 14) sent by Augustine Steward to Peterhouse, Cambridge.

1584. Left Cambridge without taking a degree.

1587. Admitted to Gray's Inn as law student.

[1] For some of these facts I depend on the authority of the Clarendon Press edition of Campion's works, by Mr. S. Percival Vivian.

1588. Took part in comedy played before Lord Burghley and other great nobles at Gray's Inn.

1587 and 1588. Deeds executed between Thomas Campion and Augustine Steward, settling up business between ward and guardian. Campion not called to bar, but continued connection with Gray's Inn up to 1595.

1591. Published five anonymous "Cantos." See text, Chapter II.

1593. Reference to Campion in George Peele's *Honour of the Garter*.

1595. *Thomæ Campiani Poemata*, Latin poems.

1596. Reference by Nashe in *Have with you to Saffron Walden*.

1597. Contributed Latin epigram to Dowland's *First Book of Airs*.

1598. Mentioned by Meres in *Palladis Thamia*.

1601. *A Book of Airs*, with Philip Rosseter. Mentioned by Fitzgeffrey in Latin epigram as second English writer of Latin epigrams, Sir Thomas More being the first. Campion in his 1595 book had claimed for himself first place.

1602. *Observations in the Art of English Poesie*.

1605. Mentioned by Camden as one of the "pregnant wits of the time."

1606. Prefatory Latin verse to Barnabe Barnes's *Four Books of Offices* by "Thomas Campion Doctor in Physic." First mention of poet as doctor. He possibly took his degree in a continental university.

1607. *A Masque in Honour of Lord Hayes and his Bride*.

1609. Prefatory verses to Ferrabosco's *Airs*.

1611. Referred to in a poem "Of London Physicians" in MS. commonplace book of a Cambridge student: "How now, Doctor Champion. . . ." (probable date). Addressed by Sir John Davies of Hereford in one of his sonnets "To Worthy Persons," appended to the *Scourge of Folly*.

Appendices

1613. *Songs of Mourning* for Prince Henry Stuart, *Masque for Marriage of Earl of Somerset, Lords' Masque, Masque for Lord Knowles, Two Books of Airs* (probable date). In this year Sir Thomas Overbury was murdered in the Tower. The murder was compassed by Robert Car, Viscount Rochester, afterwards Earl of Somerset, for whose marriage with another mover in the crime, Frances Howard, Countess of Essex, Campion composed a beautiful masque. Campion and his friend, Sir Thomas Monson, acted as agents in the sale of the lieutenancy of the Tower, which was necessary and preparatory to the plot, and so were implicated, though innocent of all share in the murder.
1614. Prefatory verses to Ravenscroft's *Brief Discourses*.
1615. Earl of Somerset in disgrace. Overbury murder brought to light. Monson committed to Tower. Campion examined but not committed. Acted as Monson's physician in Tower.
1617. *Third and Fourth Books of Airs*.
1618. *Airs that were sung and played at Brougham Castle, &c.; A New Way of making Four Parts in Counterpoint.*
1619. *Epigrammatum Libri II, Umbra, Elegiarum Liber Unus.*
1620. *Ætat.* 53, died March 1st. In his will left to Rosseter "all that he had, and wished that his estate had been far more." His estate was of the value of £22. Buried on the day of his death at St. Dunstan's in the West, Fleet Street. His friend Philip Rosseter was buried in the same place in 1623, on the 7th of May.

APPENDIX B

THE BEGINNINGS OF ENGLISH PROSODY[1]

1570. Roger Ascham: *The Scholemaster*. Reference to "reforming" movement in English verse.

1575. George Gascoigne: *Certayne Notes of Instruction in English Verse*.

1580 (?). Sir Philip Sidney: *Apologie for Poetrie* (or *Defence of Poesie*). Contains little on versification.

1580. Gabriel Harvey and Edmund Spenser: *Three Proper Wittie, Familiar Letters*, &c. A correspondence on English accent and quantity.

1582. Richard Stanyhurst: *The First Four Books of Virgil his Æneis translated*, &c. With introduction on quantity.

1585. James VI of Scotland (later James I of England): *Essays of a Prentice in the Divine Art of Poesie*. "Ane short treatise, conteining some rewlis and cautelis to be observit and eschewit in Scottis Poesie."

1586. William Webbe: *A Discourse on English Poetrie*. Campion borrowed some things from Webbe.

1588. Abraham Fraunce: *The Lawiers Logike* and *The Arcadian Rhetorike*.

1589. Puttenham: *The Art of English Poesie*. The first considerable treatise on English metric. Published anonymously.

1591. Sir John Harrington: *An Apologie of Poetrie*.

1602. Thomas Campion: *Observations in the Art of English Poesie*.

1603. Samuel Daniel: *A Defence of Ryme*.

(After this no other work of even minor importance on the subject appeared for more than half a century.)

---

[1] In this short list I have followed in the main Mr. T. S. Omond's *English Metrists*.

Appendices

APPENDIX C

OBSERVATIONS IN THE ART OF ENGLISH POESIE BY THOMAS CAMPION

(Wherein it is demonstratively prooved and by example confirmed, that the English toong will receive eight severall kinds of numbers, proper to it selfe, which are all in this booke set forth, and were never before this time by any man attempted. Printed at London by Richard Field for Andrew Wise. 1602. 8vo.)

SYNOPSIS

Dedication to Lord Buckhurst. Poetry the chief beginner and maintainer of eloquence, &c. See motto to Chapter V, *supra*. The vulgar and artificial custom of riming deters many wits from the exercise of English poesy. The writer to his book, an excellent little blank-verse poem, witty, full of gesticulation.

CHAPTER I.—Entreating of numbers in general. Number is dissevered quantity. In a poem written in number, we must consider not only the number of syllables, but their value as contained in the length or shortness of their sound. The parallel of musical notation. In verse the numeration of syllables not so much to be observed as their weight and due proportion. The art of joining words to music, long notes for long syllables, short for short. Music and poetry confounded by Terence. The dignity of classical quantitative poetry. The vulgar and easy kind of poetry now in use (rime) the birth of a lack-learning time in barbarised Italy.

CHAPTER II.—Declaring the unaptness of rime in poesy. Rime has glorious defenders, and has a kind of right of prescription. But ill uses should be abolished. Things naturally imperfect cannot be perfected by use. Old customs, if better, should be recalled. The unaptness of modern languages to the custom of "numerous" poesy and the difficulty of imitation, disheartening. The facility and popularity of rime makes many poets. Rime defined. Alliteration. The ear a rational sense and a chief judge of proportion, but in riming verse no proportion is kept, a confused inequality of syllables. Different feet confused. Rime a childish titillation abandoned by the noble Grecians and Romans. An intolerable fault of rime: "it enforceth a man oftentimes to abjure his matter and extend a short conceit beyond all bounds of art." Italians, Frenchmen, and Spaniards would prefer their rimed works translated into the ancient numbers of the Greeks and Romans.

CHAPTER III.—Of our English numbers in general. Classical measures. Failure of dactylic hexameter in English— "altogether against the nature of the language." Iambic and trochaic numbers suitable to English.

CHAPTER IV.—Of the iambic verse. To a musician able to time a song, Latin verses of six feet, heroic or iambic, or of five, as trochaic, are of same length of sound as English verses of five feet = five "sem'briefs." Examples. Rests, begotten by the heaviness of our syllables, like rests in music. Monosyllables enforce breathings, and so lengthen verse. The "iambic licenciate," English heroic verse. Examples. Must have iamb in third and fifth places. Cesura after second foot. Exceptions. (Campion's error: quantity and stress.)

CHAPTER V.—Of the iambic dimetre or English march. Consists of two feet and one odd syllable. Three examples—a chorus, a lyric, an epigram.

CHAPTER VI.—Of the English trochaic verse. Pentameter trochaic verse. Equivalence permissible once in a line. Examples, twelve witty epigrams, some of them, in spite

Appendices

of Campion's disclaimer, directed against living persons—Barnabe Barnes, Gabriel Harvey, and others.

CHAPTER VII.—Of the English elegiac verse. Example: "Constant to none . . ." See Chapter VIII of *Dissertation* Epigrams as examples.

CHAPTER VIII.—Of ditties and odes. Lyrical numbers apt to be sung to an instrument. The English sapphic. Three kinds. "Rose-cheek'd Laura" example of second kind.

CHAPTER IX.—Of the anacreontic verse. A simple number. Example: "Follow, follow." See Chapter VIII of *Dissertation*. So, eight several kinds of English numbers, simple and compound. "Ears accustomed altogether to the fatness of rime, may except against these, but . . . they close so perfectly, that the help of rime were not only in them superfluous, but also absurd." Suitability of these numbers to English. Six kinds of feet: rĕvēnge, beāutў, cōnstānt, mĭsĕrў, mĭsĕriēs, dēstĭnў.

CHAPTER X.—Of the quantity of English syllables. Greek quantity more licentious than Latin, English more so than either. Monosyllables are of heavy carriage. Accent the guide to value. Position the only impediment that can alter the accent of a syllable. In music the second syllable of *Trumpington* must be set to a long note, though "accented short." Elision. Rising and falling accent. Rules of length.

"These rules concerning the quantity of our English syllables I have disposed as they came next into my memory; others, more methodical, time and practice may produce. In the mean season, as the grammarians leave many syllables to the authority of poets, so do I leave many to their judgments; and withal thus conclude, that there is no art begun and perfected at one enterprise."

APPENDIX D

SAMUEL DANIEL AND HIS "DEFENCE OF RYME"

SAMUEL DANIEL, BORN 1562, DIED 1619.

> *Daniel, gentle, bland and good,*
> *The wisest monitor of womanhood.*
> HARTLEY COLERIDGE.

A good poet in his day and at his hour, he understood the sweetness and the gravity of English poetry. An almost impeccable metrist and rhythmist, though he had not such a command of lyrical music as Campion. GEORGE SAINTSBURY.

THE most striking thing about Daniel is the admiration in which his character has been held at all times. Courtesy was his distinguishing trait. His poetry, especially in his *Sonnets to Delia*, has generally the stately diction of the grand style. "In Daniel," says Arthur Symons, "Wordsworth found his gnomic and rational style, as of a lofty prose." Some of his prose passages have rarely been excelled in English.

Here I quote one of his sonnets and some excerpts from his *Defence*.

"SONNETS TO DELIA," NO. L (FROM EDITION OF 1594)

Let others sing of Knights and Paladines
In agèd accents and untimely words;
Paint shadows in imaginary lines
Which well the reach of their high wits records:
But I must sing of thee, and those fair eyes
Authentic shall my verse in times to come;
When yet th' unborn shall say, Lo, where she lies
Whose beauty made him speak that else was dumb.

Appendices

> These are the arks, the trophies I erect,
> That fortify thy name against old age ;
> And these thy sacred virtues must protect
> Against the dark, and Time's consuming rage.
> Though th' error of my youth in them appear,
> Suffice they show I lived, and loved thee dear.

(This sonnet is a good example of Daniel's work, and illustrates as well an influence of great importance in the poetry of Daniel and others, that of Ronsard and the Pleiade. In Sir Sidney Lee's book on the French Renaissance in England, too much is made, however, of parallels and similarities in the works of French and English poets.)

PASSAGES FROM " A DEFENCE OF RYME "

Daniel begins by referring to the verse counterpart of his tract *Musophilus*. Later he vindicates custom.

" We could well have allowed of his (Campion's) numbers, had he not disgraced our rime : which custom and nature doth most powerfully defend : custom that is before all law : nature that is above all art. Every language hath her proper number or measure fitted to use and delight, which, custom entertaining by the allowance of the ear, doth modernize and make natural. All verse is but a frame of words confined within certain measure ; differing from the ordinary speech, and introduced the better to express men's conceits, both for delight and memory. Which frame of words consisting of rithmus or metrum, number or measure, are disposed into divers fashions, according to the humour of the composer, and the set of the time. And these rhythmi, as Aristotle sayth, are similar amongst all Nations, and *e naturali et sponte fusa compositione :* And they fall as naturally already in our language as ever Art can make them ; being such as the Ear of itself doth marshall in their proper rooms, and they of themselves will not willingly be put out of their rank; and that in such a verse as best comports with the nature of our language.

"And for our Ryme (which is an excellence added to this work of measure, and a Harmony far happier than any proportion Antiquity could ever shew us) doth add more grace, and hath more of delight than ever bare numbers, howsoever they can be forced to run in our slow language, can possibly yield. Which whether it be derived of Rhythmus or of Romance, which were songs the Bards and Druids about Rymes used, and therof were called Remensi, as some Italians hold; or howsoever, it is likewise number and harmony of words, consisting of agreeing sound in the last syllables of several verses, giving both to the ear an echo of a delightful report, and to the Memory a deeper impression of what is delivered therein. For as Greek and Latin verse consists of the number and quantity of syllables, so doth the English verse of measure and accent. And though it doth not strictly observe long and short syllables, yet it most religiously respects the accent; and as the short and the long make number, so the Acute and Grave accent yield harmony: And harmony is likewise number; so that English verse then hath number, measure, and harmony in the best proportion of Music. Which being more certain and more resounding, works that effect of motion with as happy success as either the Greek or Latin. And so natural a melody is it, and so universal, as it seems to be generally borne with all the Nations of the world, as an hereditary eloquence proper to all mankind. The universality argues the general power of it; for if the Barbarian use it, then it shews that it sways the affection of the Barbarian; if civil Nations practise it, it proves that it works upon the hearts of civil Nations; if all, then that it hath a power in nature on all."

.   .   .   .   .   .

Appendices

"In an eminent spirit, whom Nature hath fitted for that mystery, Ryme is no impediment to his conceit, but rather gives him wings to mount, and carries him not out of his course, but as it were beyond his power to a far happier flight."

. . . . . .

"But yet notwithstanding all this which I have here delivered in the defence of Ryme, I am not so far in love with mine own mystery, or will seem so forward, as to be against the reformation and the better settling these measures of ours : wherein there be many things I could wish were more certain and better ordered, though myself dare not take it upon me to be a Teacher therein, having so much need to learn of others. And I must confess, that to mine own ear, these continual cadences of couplets used in long and continued Poems are very tiresome and unpleasing, by reason that still methinks they run on, with sound of one nature, and a kind of certainty which stuffs the delight rather than entertains it. But yet notwithstanding, I must not of mine own daintiness condemn this kind of writing, which peradventure to another may seem most delightful : and worthy compositions we see to have passed with commendation in that kind. Besides methinks sometimes to beguile the ear with a running and passing over the Ryme, as no bound to stay us in the line, where the violence of the matter will break thorow, is rather graceful than otherwise : wherein I find my Homer-Lucan, as if he gloried to seem to have no bounds, albeit he were confined within his measures to be in my conceit most happy : For so hereby they who care not for Verse or Ryme may pass it over with taking notice thereof, and please themselves with a well measured Prose. And I must confess my Adversary hath wrought this much upon me, that I think a Tragedy would indeed best comport with a blank Verse and dispence with Ryme, saving in the Chorus, or where a sentence shall require a couplet. And to avoid this overglutting the ear with that always certain and full incounter of Ryme, I have essayed in some of my Epistles to alter the usual place of meeting and to set it further off by one Verse, to try how I could disuse mine own ear, and to ease it of this continual burden which indeed seems to surcharge it a little too much; but as yet I cannot come to myself therein, this alternate or cross Ryme holding still the best place in my affection."

LISTS OF AUTHORITIES

A. In writing my dissertation I have made use of the following works in English :—

Alden, R. M., *English Verse* and *Introduction to Poetry*.
Arnold, Matthew, *On Translating Homer* and *Last Words on Translating Homer*.
Atkinson, Robert (Professor, Dublin University), *On Irish Metric*.
Beeching, H. C., *Two Lectures Introductory to the Study of Poetry*.
Bradley, A. C., *Oxford Lectures on Poetry*.
Broadhouse, John, *Musical Acoustics*.
Bullen, A. H., *Lyrics from the Song-Books of the Elizabethan Age* (with introduction), *More Lyrics from the Song-Books*, *Works of Thomas Campion* (Chiswick Press, 1889), *Complete English Works of Thomas Campion* (Sidgwick and Jackson, 1909).
Campion, Thomas, Works.
Chappell, William, *Old English Popular Music*, *The Song Book* (Golden Treasury Series).
Contemporary Review, November 1894.
Daniel, Samuel, *A Defence of Ryme*.
Davidson, John, Note on Poetry in *Holiday and Other Poems*.
Dodge, Janet, Note on Campion's Music in Bullen's reprint of his *editio princeps* of Campion.
Dictionary of National Biography.
Encyclopædia Britannica, Various Articles on Music, Rhythm, &c.

Thomas Campion and the Art of English Poetry

English Review, June and July 1911.

Grove, *Dictionary of Music and Musicians*.

Hueffer, Francis, *The Troubadours*.

Larminie, William, Article in *Contemporary Review*, on *The Development of English Metres* (November 1894).

Macran, H. S., Introduction to edition of Aristoxenus.

Meyer, Kuno, *Ancient Irish Poetry* and *Primer of Irish Metrics*.

Newman, F. W., *Homeric Translation in Theory and Practice*, being a reply to Matthew Arnold's Essay mentioned above.

Omond, T. S., *A Study of Metre* (Moring), *English Metrists*, and *English Metrists in the Eighteenth and Nineteenth Centuries* (Frowde).

Patmore, Coventry, *Essay on English Metrical Law*.

Quarterly Review, October 1902, and July 1911, Articles on English Prosody.

Robertson, J. M., M.P., Articles in *English Review*, June and July 1911.

Saintsbury, George, *History of English Prosody* (Macmillan), and *Manual of English Prosody* (Macmillan).

Sidney, Sir Philip, *Apologie for Poetrie*.

Sigerson, George, *Bards of the Gael and Gaul* (Introduction).

Stone, W. J., *Classical Metres in English*.

Vivian, Percival, *Poetical Works (in English) of Thomas Campion* (Muses' Library, Routledge), *Campion's Works* (Clarendon Press, Oxford).

Williams, Abdy, *The Story of Notation*.

B. I have also consulted *The Cambridge History of Literature*, *The Modern Language Quarterly*, and prose works by the following writers in English :—

Thomas Arnold, Robert Bridges, S. T. Coleridge, W. J. Courthorpe, Miss J. P. Dabney, Th. Watts-Dunton,

Lists of Authorities

Abraham Fraunce, F. B. Gummere, Dr. Guest, W. J. Henderson, Sir Sidney Lee, J. W. Mackail, Milton, Dr. Mitford, H. A. J. Munro, F. W. H. Myers (on Wordsworth), E. A. Poe, Puttenham, E. Rhys (Introduction to *Literary Pamphlets*), T. B. Rudmose-Brown, P. B. Shelley, W. W. Skeat, G. Gregory Smith, Richard Stanyhurst, R. L. Stevenson, A. C. Swinburne, J. A. Symonds, William Whewell, Wordsworth, W. B. Yeats.

From the works in List B. I have derived little or no assistance.

I omit from these lists the poetical works consulted.